5/3/03

Jules
  It's been a pleasure
working with you. I hope
you enjoy the book + gain
value from its messages —

          Best Regards

          Howard

When Goliaths Clash

When Goliaths Clash

Managing Executive Conflict to Build a More Dynamic Organization

HOWARD M. GUTTMAN

AMACOM
American Management Association
New York • Atlanta • Brussels • Buenos Aires • Chicago • London • Mexico City
San Francisco • Shanghai • Tokyo • Toronto • Washington, D. C.

This publication is designed to provide accurate and authoritative information in regard to the subject matter covered. It is sold with the understanding that the publisher is not engaged in rendering legal, accounting, or other professional service. If legal advice or other expert assistance is required, the services of a competent professional person should be sought.

Library of Congress Cataloging-in-Publication Data

Guttman, Howard M.
    When goliaths clash : managing executive conflict to build a more dynamic organization / Howard M. Guttman.
        p.   cm.
    Includes bibliographical references and index.
    ISBN 0-8144-0749-8
    1. Conflict management.   2. Organizational change.   I. Title.
HD42 .G88   2003
658.4'053—dc21   2002014674

Printing number

10   9   8   7   6   5   4   3   2   1

*To Jacqueline, my partner in life and work,
with much love and appreciation*

Contents

Preface

An organization's ability to deliver outstanding results begins with the top-management team. And while bookstore shelves are cluttered with offerings on strategy, leadership, organizational change, and performance management aimed at executives, there is little practical guidance for senior executives who want to move beyond conceptual exercises to answer the question: How can our top team—and, by extension, teams throughout our organization—perform like a winner?

Here is the short answer: Ensure that your team of senior executives is a cohesive group of fully engaged players—a mini board of directors—united in purpose and competent to act.

True enough, but the question, once again, is: How?

Coming to terms with "how" is the central aim of *When Goliaths Clash*. This book is less about conflict management *per se* and more about turning conflict within senior teams into a dynamic force for business results.

This is a tough challenge, given globalization, Digital-Age decision making, asynchronous work patterns, and the cubicalization of relationships. These centrifugal forces and many others have made organizations holding pens of dysfunctional conflict. This compromises business results and destroys morale.

Add to this the recent serial accounting shenanigans, from Adelphia to Enron to WorldCom to Xerox. At a deeper level, these revelations point to a pattern of collusion and even deceit. As a result, Wall Street is jittery; members of boards of directors are increasingly skittish; and employees are left to wonder about their leaders' values and the disturbing pattern of secretive, vest-pocket decision making: *What were all those who were involved pretending not to know?*

These events have put a premium on honest, open discussion, debate, and confrontation within organizations. Eliminating conflict is unrealistic; suppressing it only drives conflict underground. Goliaths—and Davids down the line—have little choice but to learn how to bring forward competing points of view. They must learn how to clash effectively, and this book provides a road map for doing so.

In working with senior teams in organizations of every size and type across many industries and on six continents, we have discovered that conflict management is a driving business issue. Molding your senior team into a cohesive group of fully engaged players inevitably leads you to rethink how to realign strategy, structure, and business relationships and how best to organize to make decisions at every level. Put differently, managing conflict is not merely some human resources training exercise but a way for an organization to become more competitive and accelerate business results.

The insights, approaches, and examples provided in *When Goliaths Clash* come from working with executives on the firing line. We "name names" and, wherever possible, we have avoided the blind citation. This approach provides readers with a greater opportunity to learn from real executives who have faced real challenges—sometimes making real mistakes—as they progressed to higher levels of team and business performance. It is our hope that some of the lessons we cite will enable readers to raise their level of play.

Many books on conflict management treat the issue as a bilateral exercise rather than as one connected to the larger performance environment. They tend to be technique-driven and neglect the larger organizational context in which conflict plays out.

When Goliaths Clash stands apart because it treats conflict as a business issue within the new social space of organizations, from individual to group, from hierarchical to horizontal structures, from face-to-face to electronic communication.

The chapter on e-conflict explores untraveled terrain and offers guidelines for dealing with a new set of challenges related to conflict management in an age of digital communication and decision making. *When Goliaths Clash* is intended for wide audiences of senior- and mid-level executives and managers and individual contributors. Anyone interested in improving his or her ability to manage conflict and improve performance should find value in the pages that follow.

Chapter 1, on the anatomy of conflict, explores the roots of conflict in individual perceptual differences and organizational conditions and discusses the options for effectively managing conflict.

Chapter 2 zeroes in on senior executive teams, assesses the causes of conflict within these settings, and offers ways to replace unresolved conflict with healthy disagreement.

Chapter 3 shows how to move smartly along the team-development wheel to manage conflict and, in the process, transform a team from dysfunctionality to high-performance.

Chapter 4 provides an up-close discussion of an effective process to create high-performance teams throughout an organization.

Chapter 5 goes to the heart of conflict management and discusses the portfolio of skills needed to manage individual and team-based conflict.

Chapter 6 wades into the new and often troubling waters of electronic communication and shows how to transform such communication from foe to ally in the struggle to manage conflict and improve performance.

Chapter 7 cuts through the fluff of "leadership" to assess an area curiously ignored by many writers on the subject: the role of the leader in managing conflict and driving business performance.

Please note that all quotations without other attribution come from personal interviews with the individual quoted. Sources quoted anonymously are done so to protect confidentiality.

When Goliaths Clash is written for executives on the run who are impatient with abstract theorizing and who insist on value-added reading that yields practical insights and results, *now.*

Acknowledgments

Many people helped to make this book possible, not the least of whom are the many clients from organizations around the world who gave their time to be interviewed and shared their stories and insights. This group of respected business leaders includes:

Joseph Amado	VP Information Services	Philip Morris U.S.A.
Roy Anise	VP Market Info & Planning	Philip Morris U.S.A.
Joe Campinell	President	L'Oréal Consumer Products
Michael Carey	Corporate Vice President H.R.	Johnson & Johnson
Lee Chaden	Senior VP H.R.	Sara Lee Corporation
John Doumani	President-International	Campbell Soup
Lew Frankfort	Chairman & CEO	Coach
Susan Fullman	Corporate VP & Director	Motorola
Sheila Hopkins	VP and General Manager	Colgate-Palmolive
Lois Huggins	VP of Org Development & Diversity	Sara Lee Corporation
Manuel Jessup	VP of Sara Lee Underwear, Sara Lee Socks, and Latin America North	Sara Lee Corporation
Gerard Kells	VP Human Resources	Johnson & Johnson
Paul S. Michaels	Regional President, America, for Mars, Inc.	Masterfoods, USA

Julia Nenke	Human Resources Director	Foxtel, Inc.
Patrick Parenty	Sr. VP & General Manager	Redken, U.S.A.
David Phelps	Vice President	YMCA
Jean-Paul Rigaudeau	Managing Director	Johnson & Johnson, Germany
Peter Wentworth	Vice President, Global H.R.	Pfizer Consumer Healthcare
Linda Woltz	President	Sara Lee Underwear
Anthony Zezzo	VP & General Manager, U.S. Sales & Marketing	Ortho Clinical Diagnostics, Inc.

I would also like to acknowledge the contribution of my colleagues at Guttman Development Strategies, Inc., who have been my professional family for many years. Collectively, this group has helped to shape my thinking and enabled me to grow as a consultant. They include Carol Bocchino, Robert DeSimone, Pete Elder, June Halper, Marty Kurtz, Mark Landsberg, Larry Neiman, Klaus Oebel, Thom Radice, Fred Schmitt, Steve Sperling, Linda Thompson, Barbara Weber, and Joe Wions.

Specific individuals who were interviewed, providing models and illustrative examples for the book, include Robert DeSimone, Marty Kurtz, Klaus Oebel, and Fred Schmitt. Content reviewers who provided critique, detailed suggestions, and support include Mel Benjamin, June Halper, Marty Kurtz, Mark Landsberg, Fred Schmitt, Dr. Alan Stavitsky, and Joe Wions.

Special thanks go to my executive assistant, Kathy Cannon, for her outstanding administrative support throughout this project.

I particularly want to recognize my professional mentor, Bernard M. Kessler, Ph.D., whose insights and friendship over many years have helped me to define my picture of what it means to be a consultant.

Other guiding lights whose work has influenced my perspective throughout my career are Peter Block, Werner Erhard, Albert Ellis, and Peter Drucker.

My sincere thanks go to the book team: my literary agent, Peter Tobia, and editor Dale Corey, both of Market Access, Inc. They played an essential role in turning the idea of this book into a reality. Their continued inspiration, editorial savvy, and professionalism made the writing of this book as effortless as it could have possibly been. My wife, Jackie Guttman, also deserves a thank you for her editorial assistance and contributions to the final text.

Thanks also to Adrienne Hickey at AMACOM Books for believing in this book and for her invaluable input and encouragement during the process of writing it.

I want to thank my family of origin, where I first practiced my rudimentary skills of conflict management! They include my mother, Elaine, who has been unwavering in her support; along with my sister, Karen; my brother, Steven; and my late father, Franklin.

Last, I want to thank my wife and children, who deal with my intensity on a daily basis and still remain steadfast. This group of survivors includes my son, Chuck; my daughters, Michelle and Melissa (who believed the title of this book should have been "Is There an Elephant in the Room?"); and my wife, Jackie, to whom this book is dedicated.

When Goliaths Clash

2

CHAPTER 1

Anatomy of Conflict

"By some estimates, managers spend 20% of their time in conflict or managing it. A manager who earns $60,000 will be wasting, in profitability terms, $12,000 of that salary on conflict. If your company has 10 managers, that's a $120,000 hit to your bottom line."[1]

When Jeffrey Erle took over as president of Litton Enterprise Solutions, a California-based information and technology services provider and a division of Litton Industries, he knew he was in for a stiff challenge.[2] Erle's division was a loosely formed confederation of East Coast and West Coast operations that needed to be integrated in order to provide customers with a full spectrum of services.

The problem: Both operations had about as much in common as Al Qaeda and The Salvation Army. On the West Coast, managers had been around for more than thirty years, running one line of business: call centers. They were hardworking but resistant to change, and they were led by an executive who thought that he deserved Erle's position.

The East Coast operation had been cobbled together

1

through recent acquisitions and specialized in enterprise-wide process consulting. The team was led by a general manager who believed that she should have been given the presidency. Her team was freewheeling and risk taking, and could not care less about Litton culture and tradition.

The lack of common ground had consequences. There was no communication between the two operations and no unified sense of direction. Covert sabotage was routinely waged by both camps to dilute the other side's effectiveness. And there was enough clawing and scrambling at the top of both operations to qualify for United Nations intervention. When Erle came on the scene, decision making had ground to a halt—along with sales.

A company that does not manage internal conflict will not succeed, regardless of its efforts to reengineer structures and processes, rev up sales and marketing efforts, develop and acquire new products, and dot-com the business. *When conflict is ignored—especially at the top—the result will be an enterprise that competes more passionately with itself than with its competitors.*

Not all top teams and their organizations represent conflict-ridden, Balkanized environments. But even vaunted high-performance teams are not conflict-free utopias. Unmanaged conflict at the top of an organization is especially insidious, because it can compromise the competitive well-being of an organization.

A large pharmaceutical company located in the Northeast sought to eat away at its rival's market share by launching a new product in the feminine health category. The time frame was tight because of anticipated competitive moves; however, external competition paled compared to the internal cross-pressures.

The vice presidents of marketing and research both agreed that a new product was necessary for future growth, but the question was, "Which new product to launch?" Each executive argued strenuously for a different pet alternative, and they became increasingly intransigent. The president listened to the raging debate at several board meetings, until—in an effort to end the stalemate—he decided to play Solomon. He split the product launch in half, with 50 percent of the advertising dollars and other resources going to each product. His move quelled the conflict, but with insufficient resources, neither product could be brought to market ahead of the competition. Market share was lost, and the organization's franchise in feminine health care took years to rebuild.

Unresolved conflict, especially at the highest level of an organization, can result in unfortunate, and potentially deadly, consequences, such as:

❐ Unproductive activity
❐ Misdirected anger and hostility
❐ Increased costs and waste
❐ Poor quality
❐ Reduced productivity
❐ Increased absenteeism and turnover

In our two decades of consulting, we have seen many companies that were either paralyzed by unmanaged conflict or nearly destroyed by it. Yet, for these organizations, the first thing we stress is that putting an end to conflict is the last thing executives should hope to achieve. *Conflict should be managed, not eliminated.*

The Two Faces of Conflict

The biggest misconception that people hold about conflict is that it is intrinsically bad. But conflict in and of itself is an inevitable social and organizational reality. Whether one subscribes to the Bible or to Freud, conflict is rooted in the human condition and is not necessarily an indicator of dysfunction. *It just is.*

It is true that conflict is destructive when it:

- ❐ Leads to a win/lose game where one side wins at the other's expense
- ❐ Diverts energy from important activities or issues
- ❐ Destroys people's morale
- ❐ Polarizes groups and reduces cooperation
- ❐ Deepens differences
- ❐ Produces irresponsible/regrettable behavior (i.e., personal attacks)
- ❐ Leads to stalemates rather than decisions

Conflict, however, has another side that is often overlooked. Remember the old advertisement featuring near-mythic body-builder Charles Atlas? He built an impressive physique through a process called" dynamic tension," which puts muscle against muscle. In the same way, the dynamic tension that results when executives go head-to-head can be a source of great creativity, excitement, and even strength. It can help an organization to develop the muscle it needs to vanquish less well-endowed competitors.

Takeo Fujisawa, cofounder of the Honda Motor Company, understood the positive role that conflict plays in keeping an organization vital:

> I like Bartok and Stravinsky. It's a discordant sound—and there are discordant sounds inside a company. As president, you must orchestrate the discordant sounds into a kind of harmony. But you never want too much harmony. One

must cultivate a taste for finding harmony within discord, or you will drift away from the forces that keep a company alive.[3]

Fujisawa believed strongly that examining and accepting differences is healthy, beneficial, and necessary. Probing management disagreements can spur effective problem solving and be a boon for creating strategic and operational decision making. Sharing competing viewpoints shapes and sharpens action as it opens up thinking to new possibilities. Conflict keeps a company alive—and flourishing—when it:

❏ Stimulates healthy interaction and involvement in accomplishing a task

❏ Opens up issues of importance

❏ Strengthens team spirit and generates commitment to group goals

❏ Results in greater understanding

❏ Helps to build cohesiveness

❏ Helps individuals to grow

❏ Results in better solutions to a problem

❏ Improves the quality of a group's work

Whether conflict works for or against an organization, shores it up or undermines its foundation, depends on one and only one thing: *how it is managed.*

Transforming Destructive Conflict

Think back for a moment to the situation that Jeffrey Erle walked into at Litton and to the compromise that the pharmaceutical president believed would solve a contentious problem. Until Erle came on the scene, destructive conflict was accepted as the status quo and allowed to fester. And in the pharmaceutical company, the president's split-the-baby-in-half solution killed both products. In attempting to please everyone, the president abdicated his responsibility as a leader.

In both cases no one encouraged, much less forced, the warring parties to confront one another, make their respective cases, then arrive at the solution that was best for the organization. Conflict was not mismanaged, rather it was simply never managed.

Contrast these two situations with that of Coach, a premier retailer of leather accessories. In the early 1990s, Coach's continued rapid growth was uncertain, because the company faced stiff competition not only from traditional rivals but also from several high-energy upstarts. Lew Frankfort, Coach's chief executive officer and chairman, knew that continued growth depended on strengthening the company's ability to bring new products to market more quickly and with greater consistency. The bottom line was that Frankfort needed to inject more design and merchandising muscle into his manufacturing-driven organization.

To do this, Frankfort brought on board new senior-level design and merchandizing talent. It was a terrific move, but the entrenched manufacturing group thought otherwise. The vice president of manufacturing was not only change-averse, but there were also glaring cultural differences between the forces of creativity and those responsible for getting things produced on time and cost-effectively. This led to the typical arguments and finger-pointing.

Frankfort was wise enough not to play Solomon. He confronted both groups and told them, in effect, to get their act together. He asked the warring executives and their respective teams to sit down together to honestly and openly identify the issues that divided them and to develop a plan for resolution. This was accomplished during several off-site meetings.

In addition, Frankfort asked his vice presidents of manufacturing and design to meet together on a weekly basis and then jointly produce a report for Frankfort, outlining progress on issues and highlighting areas of disagreement. Frankfort commented, "This gave me a platform to intervene only when it was absolutely necessary."

As a result, both groups began to realize that without continued collaboration the success of their company—and their jobs—was at risk. The fact that both leaders were now working together effectively, combined with the off-site meetings, broke down the silos and reduced bickering. And, best of all, new styles began to hit the shelves at regular intervals. Coach was able to maintain its rapid growth in the face of much tougher market conditions.

Another executive who knows how to bring competing energies together to achieve a positive outcome is the president of a large consumer goods company. He became president of a $1.5 billion company after it had acquired several smaller companies. His immediate challenge was to create an integrated company that would present a single face to the external world and that would run on one set of internal systems.

But a major problem stood in the way. One of the CEOs whose company had been acquired feared that his enterprise would be gobbled up by the giant, thereby losing the brand equity he had worked diligently to achieve. To preserve his company's autonomy, the CEO resisted the changes that were designed to bring his operation into the parent company's fold.

The president of the parent company proceeded to quickly put his stake in the ground. To avoid the culture clashes that were beginning to erupt with the CEO of the newly acquired company, he first created a company-wide sales team that included representatives from the larger entity and from all the acquired companies. The object was to establish a single point of contact for all the company's products. Next, he created cross-functional teams, also representing the entire organization, and charged them with developing company-wide systems for IT, accounting, ordering, and other functions. He established a clear set of goals for the teams, defined roles, and made everyone commit to a common process for decision making.

Instead of allowing unchecked internal conflict to jeopardize the company's overall health, the president quickly stepped in to create venues for collaboration. Discussion and debate were fine, and he did not attempt to dictate solutions. But by composition, structure, processes, and tasks, team members were forced to put aside parochialism and channel their differences into solutions that benefited the entire company.

By their words and actions, effective managers of conflict send the message that dissenting opinions do not need to be kept under a barrel. They not only encourage people to engage in authentic dialogue but they actually hold them accountable for doing so.

The Roots of Conflict

Conflict is the condition in which the needs or desires of two or more parties appear to be incompatible. When two or more parties vie for the same thing—whether it is money, materials, space, time, or any other resource—they are in conflict. The word *conflict* comes from the Latin *fligere* ("to strike") and *com* ("together"), so it is not surprising that one of the images that often comes to mind when we speak of conflict is that of striking or butting heads.

This negative image often brings to mind other words that evoke discomfort and struggle, such as anger, pressure, argument, enemy, disagreement, and obstacle. Vocabulary that was once restricted to the battlefield has made its way into board-rooms. People talk about "shooting down" coworkers' ideas, "coming up with a plan of attack," "rolling out the big guns," "mounting an offensive," and "dropping a bombshell." A visitor from Mars could easily get the idea that executives on this planet settle management disputes with weapons of mass destruction.

The belligerent mind-set with which people approach conflict is indicative of their belief that conflict springs from some sort of malevolent force: the serpent in the Garden of Eden, the dark side of the moon, the fundamentally flawed nature of humankind. As we pointed out earlier, this type of value judgment does conflict a great disservice. How different we would feel about conflict if we could learn to think of it as simply another expression of human diversity, which, in fact, it is.

Whenever people are brought together, each with individual needs, there exists the potential for disagreement. Conflict is inevitable, at some point, in all personal relationships and, even more so, in business transactions. In what other social institution besides business are people with different cultural backgrounds, values, and beliefs, and with different psychological needs and makeup, thrust together almost at random for eight or more hours a day, year after year, in the hope of working together to achieve a common set of objectives? It is inconceivable that all parties will consistently agree on all matters.

And business conflict is not found only among the Goliaths at the top. It is omnipresent in organizations. It transcends hierarchies, cuts across functions, and exists at that basic molecular unit of workplace reality where supervisors meet direct reports and where one employee interacts with another.

Even worse, the modern industrial enterprise, with its hyperactivity and need for business at the speed of thought, its asynchronous work patterns and global reach, and its increasing reliance on electronic communication, has become a holding pen for conflict.

Senior executives need, more than ever, to become adept at managing conflict throughout their organization. To do this, they need to understand more about the roots of conflict—in other words, the reasons that conflict is essential to the human condition.

What Causes Conflict?

There are two primary sources of conflict among people, in both their personal and business relationships: individual differences and stylistic clashes. In business relationships, a third factor contributes to the generation of conflict: organizational conditions.

Individual Differences

No two human beings—not even identical twins—are alike in all aspects. No big news here. Each person is unique, and uniqueness implies differences. As a result, all of us bring to relationships different:

- ❐ Wants and needs
- ❐ Values and beliefs
- ❐ Assumptions and interpretations
- ❐ Degrees of knowledge and information
- ❐ Expectations
- ❐ Culture

When we encounter other people whose wants and needs, values and beliefs, assumptions and interpretations differ from our own, we may find ourselves in conflict with them. But that does not mean that we must "butt heads." People can have differences without taking them personally, and *one of the keys to successfully managing conflict is learning to depersonalize it, or to view it as a business case.*

Most of the differences previously mentioned are fairly universal and easily understood. Culture, however, is a far more complicated source of conflict than the others. It may be that culture plays a pivotal role in determining how conflict expresses itself, both between individuals and in groups. Some cultures, at least stereotypically, are said to be conflict-averse, preferring to sidestep controversy to preserve peace and promote the common good. We suggest using caution with these stereotypes.

Germany is touted to be a place where, even today, leaders brook little disagreement, much less overt conflict. Recently, one group of twenty-five German managers was working on its conflict-resolution skills. The company's director of human resources described the group's leader as "harsh, rigid, and judgmental." According to this individual, anyone who wanted to help this group to improve its performance had to first understand that "Germans don't criticize their leaders. They go along with them out of respect." Given his international experience in conflict management, the facilitator leading the effort was skeptical. He knew that you cannot "respect away" conflict, although you might try to submerge it.

At the initial team meeting, the facilitator turned to the leader and advised him to be open, to admit that he valued candor, and to encourage everyone to be honest. The leader readily agreed. "What's important," he told the group, "is that we come out of here with a better sense of how we need to operate and how I can be a better leader."

This opened up the floodgates. For the first time, team members told their leader how much they resented the fact that decisions were handed to them as *faits accomplis*. They said they were tired of only being seen; they wanted to be heard. They told their leader that he needed to respect their contribution to the business. The leader not only accepted their open criticism of him but thanked them for their candor. He promised to do better in the future, thereby paving the way for a new way of interacting with them. So much for stereotypes!

Individual and Perceptual Differences

Individual differences are often the result of differences in perception. People often say that perception is reality, but in fact, perception is only a partial reality—ours and not the other person's. And it is on *our* perception that we base our wants, needs, values, beliefs, and so forth.

Perception tends to evolve in the same way for all of us. As we go through life, we accumulate *experience*—some positive, some negative. From that experience, we develop our *knowledge* base. If, for example, you have a great experience with a winning team, then you "know" that teams can accomplish more than a single contributor. But a bad experience deposits a different data point in your memory bank: You "know" that working in a team creates stress, slows down productivity, and produces mediocre outcomes.

We tend to generalize what we learn from our experiences, and these *generalizations* form our perceptions. So, if you have knowledge of a positive team experience, you might have a perception that teamwork is a good thing. Conversely, if you have knowledge of a disastrous team outcome, you might develop a negative perception of teamwork.

The Power of Going-In Stories

Perceptions create *expectations*, or *core beliefs*, about what will happen when we enter a situation similar to the one we have already experienced. These, in turn, give rise to what we call *"going-in stories."* Based on my experience, if my core belief is that teams work well, I will be more likely to enter a team situation with the going-in story that differences among team members should be viewed as constructive challenges and a way to create better goals and outcomes. If my core belief is that teams do not work well, when I see team members challenging one another I will probably tell myself the story that this is merely another example of group chaos and the outcome will likely be negative. I will probably become argumentative and defensive, thereby increasing whatever tension may already exist. In other words, I tend to look for evidence to *confirm* that my core belief/story is valid, then behave accordingly. My continued resistance to team efforts helps to perpetuate the tension in the group, which adds to my knowledge base that teams do not work, and thus the cycle repeats itself.

This process is represented in Figure 1-1:

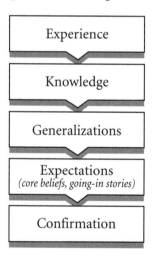

Figure 1-1. The evolution of perception.

We rely on our perceptions to guide us through our interactions with others. The trouble occurs when we act in accordance with our perceptions, but there is a disconnect between our view of things and the views of those with whom we are dealing. By not opening ourselves up to data that broadens our perspective, we become prisoners of our perceptions. Our core beliefs turn into *"core limiting beliefs,"* and by holding on to them, we lock ourselves hopelessly into ongoing conflict. Our objective becomes not to seek common ground but to prove that our perception—our core limiting belief—is the right one. To this end, we develop going-in stories that become self-fulfilling prophecies.

In a business situation, going-in stories can revolve around people's sense of self and others, their feelings about their function, or their interpretation of the organization as a whole. Recently, when the global team of a large food products corporation met to work on its conflict-resolution skills, a female executive in her forties, who had been with the company for three or four years, shared with the group her feeling that she often was not taken seriously by the others because she was viewed as being "too young" or "the new kid on the block." This perception, she revealed, often kept her from offering suggestions and giving opinions, even when she felt strongly about issues. She was taken aback when the members of the group told her that they had never considered her too inexperienced and, indeed, valued her perspective. It was her own going-in story, not the view of her colleagues, that limited her effectiveness.

People's perceptions are often limited by their positional role and are influenced by supporting systems such as the performance management and rewards processes. This sets the stage for conflict before they even begin to interact with those in other functions.

Peter Wentworth, vice president of global human resources for Pfizer's consumer health care division, illustrates this point when he discusses the perceptions of his organization's regional players:

Regional players have the potential to be very territorial. Their going-in story is that the best way to drive global growth is by growing their own region. So they attempt to optimize what they do individually. Yet, the people who run the global category are the ones who have responsibility for driving global growth. The global head of oral care, for example, will say, "This is where we need to be investing; these are the product lines that we need to grow; this is how we need to balance our global portfolio and allocate resources across the various geographies." But, given his going-in story, the regional head is likely to respond with, "I know what our customers need, and in order to meet our growth goals we are going to do 'A.' I know you want to do 'B,' but that's just not a priority for us."

Wentworth knows that it is difficult to avoid conflict when people's going-in stories are so parochial. He concludes,

Evolved team leaders know, however, that such conflict can be managed. The key: changing the going-in stories of all the individual players so that they perceive themselves first and foremost as members of a global team who share common goals and only secondarily as regional, category, or functional executives.

Sometimes an entire organization will subscribe to a going-in story about the limits that exist within the organization and the punishment that is likely to be meted out to anyone who dares to cross the line. In many cases, these stories no longer have any foundation or never did, but they are perpetuated nonetheless and can deaden creativity and morale. One vice president of marketing shared an example of this type of going-in story:

> Several years ago, we had a president who made all the calls himself and wasn't open to change. He did not allow individuals to voice their opinion, and many people were intimidated and, therefore, never challenged him. People who did weren't very successful. As a result, there was a lot of fear about speaking up. Today, even though we have had two presidents since he left and our current president has done a lot to encourage candor, we still hear stories about people being afraid to speak their mind. When you begin to drill down and try to understand what it is all about, why it exists, you find out that it has to do with the way people were managed then. But it held us back until we were able to successfully work through our stories.

There is a way to avoid being trapped by your going-in story: Use the input of others to build, modify, test, and perhaps abandon perceptions. By asking other people for their opinions and by probing how those opinions were formed, we open ourselves up to entirely new ways of looking at the people and events around us.

To successfully manage conflict we must also be willing to share our perceptions with others—to tell them exactly what we value and what we expect from them. Only when each party opens up to the other, revealing their perceptions, can conflict be resolved—which brings us to the second factor that often generates conflict: stylistic clashes.

Stylistic Clashes

If you master the skill of sending and receiving clear messages, you hold a key to forging successful relationships, from marriage to the workplace.

Communication may be the one area where style is not only sizzle but substance. When we talk about style, we are referring to how each individual approaches interpersonal communication. Some people are comfortable revealing their innermost thoughts and feelings, while others find it extremely awkward and embarrassing to open up, especially in front of a group. The fight-like-cats-and-dogs-and-then-kiss-and-make-up style works for many couples—and many business partners—while others are appalled by such unabashed displays. Our style of interacting with other people can often be traced back to our ethnic roots. In Australia and the United States, greeting a business acquaintance with a slap on the back and a "How ya been?" is perfectly acceptable. But do not try backslapping in Japan!

Effective communication is critical for resolving differences, and each one of us needs to be aware of how we communicate. What is our primary style? Do we use it some, all, or most of the time? Do we vary our style depending on the situation? The person we are currently communicating with? The issue that is on the table?

Although human behavior does not lend itself to neat typologies, we have found it helpful to think about the method we use to communicate in terms of three broad styles: *nonassertive, assertive,* and *aggressive.* We will discuss the three styles—and how a person can move among them—in detail in Chapter 5, but we would like to point out here that one of the toughest tasks is accurately identifying your own personal style.

For example, one important exercise that occurs during a conflict-resolution session involves asking the team members, one by one, to pinpoint where on the continuum from nonassertive to assertive to aggressive they believe their behavior generally falls. The facilitator then asks each of the other team members to comment on the person's self-assessment. The results are often revealing.

On one high-level cross-functional team, a manager named Dan rated himself highly assertive, as represented by the x on the behavioral continuum shown in Figure 1-2.

When the rest of the team discussed Dan's self-assessment, it quickly became apparent that there was a fairly large disconnect between his image of himself and theirs. The majority of the group said that they considered Dan to be very aggressive. They pointed to his intensity and the fact that he was "wound tight." They said that when he presented his viewpoint he was not open to discussion or critique. One or two of his colleagues confessed that they felt intimidated by Dan. The group's average assessment of Dan is represented by the y at the far right of the continuum.

	x		y
Nonassertive	Assertive		Aggressive

Figure 1-2. The behavioral continuum.

Dan was surprised by the disconnect between his assessment of himself and that of the group, and this gave him new insight into the way he was communicating with other people. It is not always easy to see ourselves as other people see us, but until we do, our perceptions will remain limited—and limiting.

The behavioral continuum applies not only to individual managers but also to organizations. In one Northeast-based financial organization, for example, the culture was squarely on the far right (or aggressive) side of the continuum. When the organization implemented a new performance-management system, the divisional CEOs knew that they needed to move toward becoming more collaborative. This meant abandoning the winner-take-all mentality that had long characterized their behavior. The biggest challenge, it turns out, was getting the CEOs' team members to express their legitimate differences of opinion with their leaders. For too long, they had been cowered into submission.

By discussing the behavioral continuum, the CEOs quickly saw that different behaviors on the continuum can have very different consequences. For example, the overarching aggressive style of the CEOs had led to the formation of underground resistance armies that had quietly sandbagged divisional decisions. With this insight, the CEOs moved to a less aggressive, but more assertive point on the continuum and this, in turn, led to more open and honest discussion and debate.

Organizational Conditions

The conditions under which we work can be a significant conflict producer. Hierarchical structure, policies and procedures, performance reviews, reward systems, organizational culture, and even physical plant conditions can, on occasion, turn even the mildest-mannered employee into a raging bull.

Adding to the stress is the fact that today's companies are matter in motion, to paraphrase Thomas Hobbes. Downsizing, rightsizing, restructuring, reengineering, delayering—you name it—continue on as an unending parade of changes within most organizations. This constant churn increases the potential for disagreement. Executives frequently find themselves competing for resources, clarifying roles and procedures, setting standards, and establishing goals and priorities. Change, by its very nature, tends to put the status quo on trial. No sooner are resources allocated, roles clarified, and goals established then along comes a new change initiative, and the wrangling begins anew.

Conflict: Red-Hot or Cool?

Conflict is a multifaceted phenomenon. It can be manifest or latent, overt or hidden. Manifest conflict is in-your-face disagreement. It occurs when executives square off at a committee meeting or when someone comes into your office complaining loudly about next year's budget. Latent conflict is submerged disagreement. It occurs when people sit quietly through meetings plotting ways to sabotage their teammates when they walk out of the room. It exhibits itself indirectly, through lack of cooperation between departments or procrastination on project deadlines.

Take, for example, a group of Chinese engineers from a consumer goods company in Shanghai. The team faced a raft of issues: Its decision-making process was downright cryptic; its manager never asked for anyone's input; no one knew who was responsible for what; and a few extroverts dominated team meetings.

Did the engineers remain passive and stoically endure the dysfunctional environment? Not on your life! Although conflict never became manifest, it bubbled just below the surface. Some engineers offered the proverbial cold shoulder to colleagues. Other avoided interaction with fellow team members. And those who dominated the airwaves often found that their requests for support were blatantly ignored. The latent effects of not confronting conflict, it turned out, were not covert.

Whether conflict remains latent or is put on the table so there is a chance that it can be managed depends in large part on the culture of the organization—and on the signals sent down by the senior management team. The example of the German team is instructive: When the leader signaled that disagreement was healthy, his employees obliged by providing candid feedback.

Conflict and the Fear Factor

Ah, the family reunion. It is a time for relatives to reconnect and rebond. But pity those family members who fail to attend. Inevitably, they become targets of complaints and friendly fire.

The conversation is all too familiar. Someone relates the story about an absent relative's behavior, which he found to be offensive. There is considerable speculation about the relative's motivation, and then the behavior is interpreted in light of that presumed motivation. A guilty verdict is pronounced, everyone agrees, and the group moves on to the next absentee.

The point is clear: We are not comfortable, and even fear, dealing straight up with conflict. We are taught to run away from conflict: "to turn the other cheek," "to let sleeping dogs lie," and that "if you don't have something nice to say, don't say anything." And so we retreat to the least-trying option, which is turning to third parties for temporary relief.

Fear is a killer of effective conflict management. Ineffective managers of conflict are afraid of the consequences of bringing highly charged issues out into the open. They do not encourage people to speak up, to share their opinions, to tell it—and to be told—like it is. And by their refusal to discuss certain issues, they create an implicit environment that devalues authentic discussion and promotes subterfuge and double-dealing.

Options for Coping with Conflict

When you think about it, there are essentially four ways in which the players in a conflict-laden situation can deal with it:

1. *Play the victim*—Say nothing, act powerless, and complain.

2. *Leave*—Physically remove oneself from involvement.

3. *Change oneself*—Move off one's position, shift one's view of the other party, or "let it go."

4. *Confront*—Address the issue openly, candidly, and objectively; communicate with the other party.

Playing the victim is corrosive and often subversive. It leads to griping and sniping and tends to drive conflict underground. Playing the victim saps an organization of its vitality, as victims focus inward on their unresolved issues and reach out to recruit supporters to their point of view.

Let's face it. Walking away or *leaving* is always an option. We can turn our back on our friends, get divorced, or quit our job and head for greener pastures. But how many times can you run away? It is better to learn how to handle conflict.

Sometimes we can *change ourselves* by changing our perceptions of a situation. For example, you might try to achieve a positive outcome by changing your "story" or interpretation of another person's behavior.

Changing stories works successfully for some people, including the CEO whose company was acquired by the large consumer goods company, which was mentioned earlier. His original going-in story—"Beware the corporate giant"—put him on the defensive and kept him from taking advantage of the opportunities to leverage resources offered by the larger organization.

However, when he saw how effective the company president's cross-functional teams were, the CEO began to realize how self-defeating his story had been. Keeping the giant at bay might satisfy—at least temporarily—the need for autonomy, but it would not contribute to future growth and prosperity. The way to achieve these goals was to develop a cohesive sense of teamwork within his organization, to become more of a player within the corporate entity, and to confront issues relating to his unit by thrashing them out openly and honestly with his colleagues in corporate.

With this new story, he followed the president's example, creating cross-functional teams within his organization and training them in conflict-resolution skills. Now, when his team needs to take a stand vis-à-vis a corporate issue, the CEO negotiates with the parent company with greater confidence. He knows that his team speaks with one voice, that he has forged relationships with key executives higher up on the corporate ladder, and that he has the skills to advance his point of view.

Another successful story-changer is the executive vice president of a personal care company, who happens to be a person of color. After the turnover in her division began to rise, she was sent for personal coaching. It soon became apparent that the major problem was in her style: She was viewed as a model of efficiency who was disconnected emotionally. When her coach suggested that she try to show a more human side, to relate to people emotionally as well as intellectually, she countered with her story: "People are always uncomfortable around someone who's different from them. They feel disconnected from me because I am a woman and an African-American. This is always going to put me at a disadvantage in the relationship game, no matter what I do."

The coach's response to her was, "That's your story. Your story is that race plays a role in this, and that's a story you need to let go of." And she did. She realized that she alone had created her story, without any empirical evidence. Once she replaced this negative story with one story that said, "They are as comfortable with me as they are with anyone else," she was able to focus on the real issues and attain a higher level of impact. But make no mistake about it. This option may come with a price, especially if changing your perceptions entails compromising basic values, having needs go unfulfilled, or bending reality.

The option of changing oneself can be an effective tool for minimizing stress and increasing effectiveness. But what happens at those moments of truth, when all the attempts to reframe your perceptions simply do not work? The only option left is to confront conflict.

The fourth option, *confronting* conflict directly, is ideal. We like to use a colorful metaphor for allowing disagreement and conflict to go unresolved: It is like having a dead elephant's head in the middle of the room. The elephant head is unsightly, distracting, and takes up a lot of space, but no one is willing to acknowledge that it is there. Trying to ignore it distracts members of the team from focusing externally on markets, customers, and competitors. The longer the elephant head remains, the worse its effect will be—and it is unlikely that the elephant head will get up and leave. Only when team members acknowledge that the distasteful object is there and needs to be dealt with will they be able to remove it. By ending the conspiracy of silence, they can arrive at a solution for sweeping it away, giving it a proper burial, and moving on to activities that are more productive.

When thinking about figurative dead elephant heads, one team immediately comes to mind. Its problem was a minority executive in the finance division. The executive had been with the company for twenty years and lacked the managerial skill to be effective and, as a result, the organization's diversity efforts floundered. His colleagues tiptoed around this "dead elephant head." They feared that, because of his long tenure, the executive was untouchable. Consequently, they avoided confronting him. The situation deteriorated. As executives throughout the organization learned to work around their colleague, they began to show him less respect. Eventually, the executive was terminated, and away went the dead elephant head. If the issue had been confronted honestly and openly from the outset, however, it could have been resolved much sooner and without the prolonged agony.

Outing Conflict

Confronting conflict head-on is one of the hardest things an organization will ever do. To do so, executives must first puncture the many myths that exist about conflict. Most people believe that conflict is caused by contentious people—congenital malcontents who cannot or will not change; that teamwork requires a conflict-free environment; that people cannot separate disagreements over business issues from personal attacks; and that confronting another person or group always leaves bad feelings. But not one of these myths addresses a fundamental truth about conflict: It is and always will be.

Conflict must be brought out into the open and confronted. Left alone, elephant heads will rot and contaminate the organization's performance. John Doumani, president-international, Campbell Soup, put it best:

> In every organization, the important business issues are talked about behind closed doors, in the corridors, and in other places where senior management can't hear. It worries me when you meet to discuss an issue and everyone says, "Yes, yes," then walks down the corridor whispering, "That was a bunch of nonsense; it will never work." They are whispering because they fear that if they say it out loud, their heads will roll. What every company needs to do is make it okay for those corridor conversations to happen in

the formal environment: in the meeting rooms and in the boardroom. Because, inevitably, those corridor conversations tend to be right. To do so, senior management must constantly reinforce, and demonstrate, that it's okay to raise those issues, that in fact it's obligatory to do so—and that you are a "player" if you do.

Effective executives like Doumani take conflict out of the closet and treat its resolution as an opportunity to build deeper, more productive business relationships. The key issue is how to put disagreements on the table so that the executives involved can work toward the best resolution without destroying relationships. Resolving this issue is the key challenge, which the remainder of this book will address.

Testing Your Conflict-Management I.Q.

How effectively is conflict being managed in your organization? The more questions to which you answer yes, the greater your organization's need to examine its behavior and take corrective actions.

- ❐ Is your business strategy fuzzy or unclear? Does the senior team frequently debate its meaning?
- ❐ Do people arrive for meetings late or not at all?
- ❐ Do meetings frequently devolve into chaos?
- ❐ Do meetings multiply because closure is never reached?
- ❐ Does the atmosphere become tense when a certain executive enters the room or a particular issue is raised? Can you feel the tension?

conflict within their executive committee by running away from it and building firewalls around functions to keep fellow senior executives at bay. Not surprisingly, work down the line became highly fragmented. Cross-functional business processes were almost nonexistent. Work moved across boundaries haphazardly and in fits and starts. Problems were rarely resolved between functions, even when there was sufficient information to resolve them.

Typically, when product development had an issue with marketing, the issue was sent up the chain of command to the vice president of product development to be messaged further by him. He then sent it back down to his team for further comment, whereupon the issue was once again recirculated upward. Finally, the vice president of product development would meet with his counterpart in marketing for a discussion. In our estimate, such yo-yoing stymied decision making by more than 50 percent.

The top team of a multinational beauty and health care company put a premium on creating what it termed an affiliative environment, in which everyone played as a team member. Employees down the line followed the lead and adhered to the conflict-averse culture. Political correctness triumphed over issue resolution, leaving unresolved key issues that required confrontation.

Directional Discord

Strategic conflict—disagreement at the top over the future direction of the organization—is conflict at its deadliest. A few years ago, a major oil company's Canadian operation was floundering. Amid fierce competition, sales were down. The profits that were needed to fund exploration had evaporated.

Each time the president met with his senior team, sparks flew. Each executive vice president viewed his or her function as being the key to the organization's future strategic success. Not surprisingly, debate raged around resource allocation as each vice president argued adamantly for a bigger piece of the action.

The president was a veteran oilman whose idea of growth was to simply keep digging—to find as much oil as possible and sell it at the highest price the market would bear. The vice president of production had a different idea of how to grow the company—and power his own career. His ambitions centered on petrochemicals, and he envisioned himself at the head of an empire of chemical plants. The vice president of marketing and sales argued that, because of its superior distribution network, the company could easily move a variety of products, in addition to oil, into the marketplace.

Predictably, the senior team's confusion about the company's strategic thrust cascaded down through the organization. The competition for resources at the top was mirrored in similar firefights among the functional and regional directors, with each lobbying for the lion's share. There was constant clawing for the company's top talent, with department heads literally raiding one another's functions for the best people. Priorities were defined not by an overarching business strategy but by the self-interest of those heading up the silos. One production manager, for example, felt perfectly justified in saying, "If I'm going to grow production, I'm going to need the most talented people, even if that means poaching talent from other areas." This was a case of robbing Peter to shore up Paul.

And, with no clear direction from above, support functions were unable to prioritize their services. From information services (IS) to human resources, the squeaky wheel and power politics were the engines that drove resource-allocation decisions.

The uncontained internal conflict migrated beyond the

company's borders. Relations with the national and provincial governments became strained, as regional executives issued contradictory statements about the company's short- and long-term intentions.

Eventually, the company achieved a turnaround, but not until it developed a clear strategic direction and an aligned top team did it move from being a fragmented environment to become an integrated, competitive force.

It's About Strategy, Stupid

Strategic conflicts among Goliaths are not only the most deadly but also the hardest to resolve. Most senior managers simply do not have a great depth of experience in setting strategy, much less resolving directional disagreements. Most upwardly mobile managers, after all, have been rewarded for their superior operational accomplishments rather than for their strategic prowess.

Figure 2-1 depicts how the skill set required by managers changes on the way up the corporate ladder.[1]

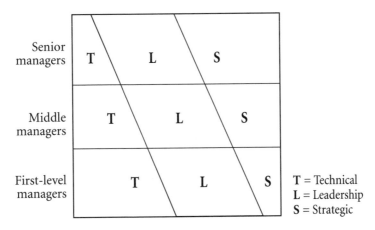

Figure 2-1. Required management skills.

First-line supervisors typically have little, if any, strategic responsibility. Although they are expected to demonstrate a certain degree of leadership ability—whether on the assembly line, in the sales office, or at the help desk—they have generally been promoted because of their excellent technical and operational skills.

Supervisors who move into middle management are expected to be not only technically proficient but to possess stronger leadership skills and some understanding of, and responsibility for, implementing company strategy.

Most managers who reach the executive suite do so because they have demonstrated operational success, technical knowledge, and the leadership skills needed to motivate others. But, the higher they climb, the less need they have for hands-on operational skills and technical knowledge, and the more they are required to think strategically beyond the current product-market configuration to the next round of competitive advantage. For many executives, this is a significant challenge. They arrive in the ranks of senior management wondering how to ensure that their organization is not only well run but also well directed.

Resolving Strategic Conflict

Ensuring the success of the organization's business strategy should be the number-one priority of every senior team. Strategy is an organization's self-definition of the future. Disagreement among senior players about future product and market scope and emphasis, key capabilities, financial targets, and growth expectations creates fault lines among senior-team members that can undermine the foundation of the business. Since this book is not about how to formulate strategy, the question we will examine is: How can a senior team resolve the conflict that keeps it from delivering the results its board and stockholders expect?

Effective conflict management begins with *alignment.* To operate at peak performance, a senior team must be aligned, or reach agreement, around four distinct factors. (See Figure 2-2.)

First, strategic goals and the key operational goals that flow from them must be clear, specific, and agreed-upon. Second, the roles of the team members need to be carefully delineated so that they know exactly what they are responsible for and what they are authorized to do. Third, protocols or ground rules must be established to guide group behavior. Finally, interpersonal relationships—the range of personal styles that members of the team adopt when interacting with one another—must be understood and managed.

Let's examine how, by becoming aligned around each of these factors, a senior team can replace unresolved conflict with healthy disagreement.

Figure 2-2. Key alignment factors.

Goals/Business Priorities/Focus

Not every senior management team is as misaligned as that of the Canadian oil company. Johnson & Johnson's senior team is a notable example of a tightly aligned, highly effective leadership group.

Johnson & Johnson (J&J) is a portfolio organization consisting of 195 companies that make up the health care giant. The companies, or business units, are organized into approximately twenty franchise groups with products as disparate as vision, skin, and feminine health care; minimally invasive surgery; wound management and closure; and drug therapies such as over-the-counter analgesics, anti-infectives, and painkillers.

Because each franchise is unique, each year J&J's senior team asks the leaders of each franchise to develop their own strategic plan, which is submitted to the executive committee for review and approval. Once the plan is approved, it is up to the individual franchise to translate the strategy into operational goals and action plans in each of its businesses, at every level.

How does J&J manage the centrifugal forces that are typically at play in a portfolio environment? According to Michael Carey, corporate vice president of human resources for J&J, the franchise strategies are tied together by clear, common goals and values, which minimize the possibilities for misunderstandings and misalignment. These goals are articulated in two places. The first is the parent company's Statement of Strategic Direction, which says that it will abide by the ethical principles of its Credo, capitalize on its decentralized form of management, and manage for the long term. The second is a list of four imperatives that have been identified by the executive committee. These imperatives of innovation, process excellence, e-business, and flawless execution are the themes around which J&J expects each of its businesses to pursue its individual strategy.

And, just as each franchise keeps the statement of strategic direction and the four imperatives in mind as it develops its strategic plan, so must the business units within the franchise as they develop theirs. Carey cites an example:

> Ethicon is one of the cornerstone companies in our wound care franchise. Its base business is wound closure: sutures, stapling, adhesives. Wound care has declared that its goal is to become the innovation leader in its category. For the franchise's strategy to succeed, the Ethicon team must be committed to the same goal. For example, R&D might suggest pursuing the me-too solution of using synthetic skin to close wounds. Marketing might respond with, "No, we need to be more innovative. We need to develop sutures and staples that cause less trauma as they pass through the skin, that produce less swelling and promote faster healing, less chance of infection, and fewer doctor visits." If the team is truly aligned around the goal of becoming an innovation leader, the choice should be an easy one. That's how having clear goals, from top to bottom, reduces the potential for in-fighting and competition among functions.

Philip Morris U.S.A. (PMUSA) is another example of a strategically aligned organization. PMUSA's senior management team focused everyone in the company around a clearly stated mission: "To be the most responsible, effective, and respected developer, manufacturer, and marketer of consumer products, especially products intended for adults. Our core business is manufacturing and marketing the best-quality tobacco products available to adults who choose to use them." The team then translated this mission statement into specific, achievable strategic and key operational goals.

These actions won the respect of Joe Amado, PMUSA's vice president of information services and chief information officer. Amado felt that the top team had provided his department with unambiguous guidance for decision making.

Unfortunately, Amado was less impressed with the stated mission of information services, which was "to transform the way people work." What linkage did this have to the company's mission statement? He was even more troubled by the vagueness of the charter and his inability to tie it to his customers' needs.

Complicating matters was the fact that IS was a department in flux. It had gone through numerous restructuring efforts, under a number of leaders, before Amado came on the scene. Amado approached his boss Roy Anise, the senior vice president of planning and information, with the idea of taking IS through the same type of alignment that had been done for Anise's own senior team. Anise agreed.

Amado assembled his direct reports—IS account directors for operations, finance, HR, marketing, and sales—and three individuals who provided services to them—the chief technology officer, the head of shared services, and leader of the project-management group. He also invited to the alignment session four senior leaders within the IS organization who, although they did not report directly to him, provided vital support to his senior team.

In their first alignment session, Amado and his team made reasonable progress on issues related to interpersonal style and accountabilities, but their lack of common goals soon became apparent. To move ahead, Amado's team needed to rethink its mission.

After several intense strategy-setting sessions, the group came up with a new mission statement: "The role of information services is to maximize our clients' contribution to the PMUSA mission by optimizing their use of information technology for business success."

With this new, clear mission in mind, Amado and his team moved to become more customer-centric. Knowing that structure should follow strategy, they decided that the best way to accomplish this was to create customer teams, so that each internal customer—marketing, finance, sales, operations, or HR—would have its own group of IS professionals who would be dedicated to helping it optimize its use of information technology (IT) to maximize its contribution to the PMUSA mission.

The customer teams were formed, and each, in turn, went through its own strategy session, setting goals consistent with the larger IS strategy and making specific action plans to help its internal customer maximize its contribution to the PMUSA mission. At PMUSA, there is a clear line of strategic sight, from senior management to IS and then to IS's internal customers.

Individual Roles/Accountability

Ending the Turf Wars

People often gripe about having too much responsibility, but try to take some of it away and you'll be amazed at how hard they fight to hold on to the status quo. Most executives equate responsibility with power—and both with pay and glory. This explains the frequent tugs-of-war that arise when corporate roles and responsibilities are not clearly delineated.

When the senior team fails to clearly delineate which function is responsible for which steps, especially in organizations where the value chain is complex, open warfare often ensues. Paul Michaels is regional president, America, for Mars, Inc., the consolidated domestic unit of Masterfoods USA's pet, snack, and food divisions, previously known as Kal Kan, M&M/Mars,

and Uncle Ben's. Considered a creative thought leader, Michaels has led teams at some of the nation's leading consumer packaged goods companies, including Johnson & Johnson and Procter & Gamble. He recognizes the importance of individual roles and accountability. Based on his years of experience, Michaels describes some of the turf battles that typically occur when a company fails to make accountabilities clear:

> Manufacturing is driven by efficiency and likes to perfect one product spec for all customers. Sales, on the other hand, is under pressure from significant clients to provide customized products. The VP of sales promises the customized products, and his or her counterpart in marketing encourages that group to begin advertising the variations. Or R&D comes up with a complicated design that strains manufacturing's resources. As complaints emerge, the VP of manufacturing makes the call to change some of the specifications. Everyone is pulled in different directions, and, before you know it, it can be all-out war.

The way to deal with this lack of alignment is to hold a formal session on the subject with the senior team. Before beginning the alignment session, it is useful to ask participants to rate the team's performance in several areas. Ask the following two questions: "How clear are you about *your* role/accountability on the team?" and "How clear are you about the *other team members'* roles/accountability?" Many CEOs and presidents are surprised and easily frustrated when they learn the scores on these questions, which are generally low. A typical retort is: "What do you mean, the head of sales isn't clear about what he does? He's in charge of sales. What's unclear about that?"

What these leaders fail to realize is that none of their team members operate in a vacuum: They are constantly bumping up against one another, passing the baton from one to another. Yet, they may have never sat down and discussed what they expect from one another at these intersection points. In many cases, the alignment session is the first time senior-team members have ever addressed these issues together.

We suggest probing further. During an alignment session, ask team members to define their job for the rest of the group, to list the activities that they carry out and the results that they are responsible for, to describe how they believe their job is perceived by other players, and to identify the gaps that exist between themselves and the other team members. Then record their responses on a matrix that is visible to the entire team. As each executive's data is added, the disconnects become increasingly apparent. The discussion that follows often results in an entirely new model, with new intersection points, on which everyone can agree.

In the course of clarifying their strategy, it became apparent to Joe Amado and his senior team that they were also unclear about their respective roles and responsibilities. For instance, Amado's direct reports, the five directors, had never really been held accountable for a specific business area, such as operations, marketing, sales, finance, or HR. Several wore multiple hats. The technology director, for example, was not only chief technology officer, accountable for all the technology across PMUSA, but he was also accountable for providing all the technology solutions to the large department known as operations. Both marketing and sales, which at the time were implementing an IT–heavy initiative, came under the umbrella of the marketing director.

The team's next step, after clearly defining each of the customer groups it was committed to serving, was to assign a director to each group. Amado explained,

> I now have five directors, and each one is aligned
> with a specific business area. That's their unique
> role. They have no other role but that. It's very
> clear to them that their performance will be
> judged by the business value they add to that
> area, the level of customer satisfaction in that
> area, and the employee satisfaction among the
> individuals that work for them.

Amado has also put in place a system to measure the results achieved by each director and his team. His scorecard is a simple, yet highly effective measurement tool. It adds discipline to the equation and reinforces responsibilities and accountability. Each of the five teams maintains a one-page "eye chart" that lists all the projects it is currently working on. Each project is then divided into three aspects: scope (i.e., the requirements for the project, what must be done to deliver business value), budget, and schedule. Progress in each area is represented by a color-coded symbol, similar to a traffic light: green indicates that it is safe to move forward; yellow means that there are some issues, and caution is called for; and red means you better stop and think about what you are going to do next.

In a large area, such as operations, IS may be involved in as many as fifteen projects at any one time. The scorecard allows Amado and his operations director to instantly assess the team's progress on all of them. If a project is falling behind schedule, the yellow symbol serves as a trigger for discussing possible solutions: Should some of the team's resources be diverted from another project to help out on this one? Is the delivery date realistic, or should it be reconsidered?

Amado's eye chart is designed to measure his teams' performance in the first category, which is the business value they add to their assigned area. But he is also holding them accountable for results in two other areas: customer and employee satisfaction. These results are also being measured, with questionnaires being sent to both groups on a regular basis and the responses tabulated and factored into performance evaluations.

Since aligning his team around a new strategic vision, Amado has noticed many changes in their behavior—as well as in his own. Much of the recurring, energy-draining conflict that once existed has finally been resolved, and the team members have become much more adept at handling new disputes when they arise:

> Complaining to others about someone else, in staff meetings and one-on-one conversations, has stopped. Now, when there are conflicts, people go right to the individual they are having a problem with and resolve it themselves. I am not getting involved in all of the minor issues that I used to, because they don't come to me anymore. They know they are accountable for solving these problems. Now they come to me only with the strategic issues, those that relate to the running of the business or issues in the marketplace.

Stopping the Buck

While amassing power is a familiar pastime in many senior management teams, so is passing the buck. And when it isn't clear who is accountable for what, that is rather easy to do.

At one manufacturing company, a new president came on board in April 2000. The company's operating plan for 2000 had been put into place in January, under his predecessor, and was predicated on the amount of product that had been shipped in 1999 rather than on what had been sold by retailers. The problem was that 1999 was an anomalous year, during which the threat of Y2K snafus fueled an unusual buildup of inventory. In addition, the company's major competitor was in bankruptcy, which caused it to project increased sales. When the new president arrived, retailers still had large stocks of excess inventory, and the company was operating under a plan that was inflated by $75 million.

The new president needed to remedy the situation, and quickly. But he could not do it alone; he needed the cooperation of the various functions to develop and execute a new plan. This was not easy to accomplish, however, because of the way in which planning had always been done and the resulting reluctance of the players to take responsibility for a new plan. He describes the situation in these words:

> Everyone on the senior team should have been involved in putting that plan together. But, in fact, only three or four people had provided the data for the original 2000 plan. The others hadn't been asked for their opinion, and they hadn't volunteered it. There were several individuals on the team who could—and should— have raised a red flag and said, "Folks, should we not look at what sold through?" Obviously, the VP of sales could have done that; the forecasting guy could have come forward and said, "Wow, we are doubling our sales potential here. What is going on?" But no one considered it his or her role, and when performance reviews were conducted, no one could be held accountable.

In light of these needs, the alignment process for the new president and his team emphasized strict accountability. Now, when the company puts together an annual operating plan, the three or four people who are responsible for projecting sales growth are expected to be able to fully explain to the rest of the team the process by which they reached the numbers. And they are questioned unremittingly until their peers are satisfied that they have covered all the bases.

Along with this new accountability, the president has instituted a new decision-making model. Before making any major decision, the team comes to an agreement as to how it is going to be made: unilaterally, collaboratively, or by consensus. Who will be consulted for information? For opinions? Who will make the final decision? And, who will execute it? Today, whether the senior team is considering a new product introduction, thinking about increasing manufacturing capacity, or contemplating the consolidation of functions, this decision-making process is adhered to.

One of the company's vice presidents gives this hypothetical example of how a consultative decision might be made under the new regime:

> Let's say that next year we make a decision to freeze salaries, across the board, for four months. Sam [the president] would say to me, "Take the lead on this," and I would work with Tom, our CFO. But other senior-team members might express the desire to be on the team with us. To them, Sam would say quite clearly, "You can provide input, but Margaret and Tom have the responsibility for making the decision. And once the decision has been made, everyone on the team will get behind it, whether they agree or disagree."

Protocols/Rules of Engagement

Clarity of goals and roles will only get you so far. Protocols for resolving conflicts—think of them as ground rules for behavior—both within the team and in its interactions with others, are the third key element in the conflict-management equation.

Team-Based Protocols

At one Johnson & Johnson subsidiary, the president proved to be an adept conflict manager. Cathy Burzik, president of Ortho Clinical Diagnostics, Inc., had her top team lay out "rules of engagement" for itself that covered everything from depersonalizing issues to keeping discussions focused on actual behaviors and what was actionable, rather than on a weather report–type of commentary that did not specify the behavior that needed to be modified or changed.

At Johnson & Johnson and elsewhere, teams have found the following protocols especially efficacious in conflict management:

❒ *Don't triangulate.* Triangulation entails bringing an issue to a third-party rescuer for resolution. Lois Huggins, former vice president of HR at Bali Company and current vice president of organizational development and diversity for Sara Lee Corporation, explains that triangulation is an attempt to avoid responsibility by using a surrogate to handle an issue that should be resolved head-on between two people. Figure 2-3 illustrates the concept of triangulation.

"When one executive on the team had an issue with another team member, he or she would often go to Chuck Nesbit (Bali's president), rather than deal directly with that colleague," Huggins says. "Chuck would then become involved and assume responsibility for getting resolution."

In another case, a member of the senior team of a property management company had outstanding technical knowledge of construction and had been with the company for many years. He had a close relationship with the president, and whenever

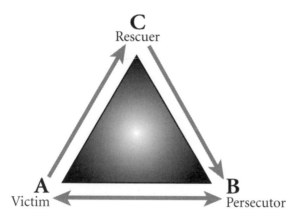

Figure 2-3. The triangulation trap.

he had an issue with another member of the team, he took his complaint straight to the president's office. The president continued to allow this dysfunctional behavior, giving the excuse that, "He's a quirky guy, but he does great work, and he was there for me in the early days."

Triangulation continued until the team went through an alignment. During the session, other members of the team expressed their displeasure with this individual's continuing attempts to co-opt the president. The president listened and then agreed that he would no longer put this person's needs above the good of the group. He promised to stop fostering this person's triangulation efforts, and he has kept that promise.

Paul Michaels is another leader who recognizes how crucial effective conflict-resolution skills have become for today's successful executives. It is a necessary skill that he fosters within his teams. He encourages direct resolution between executives with opposing points of view, without his involvement. When an executive comes to him with a complaint about a peer, Michaels insists that the complainant meet directly with that person to resolve the issue. Only if this proves ineffective will Michaels step in to coach the executives through the issues.

Michaels's insistence that the parties in conflict remain accountable not only avoids the pitfalls of triangulation but also provides those involved with an important and valuable learning opportunity.

❐ *Don't recruit supporters to your point of view.* We all know people whose main mission in life seems to be advancing their own cause. For them, life is a zero-sum game. They are always looking for opportunities to win people over to their side, and take the attitude that "if you're not with me, you're against me." They make their private disagreements public by bad-mouthing anyone who dares to contradict them.

This form of third-party recruiting is contrary to effective conflict management: it is not conducive to open, candid discussion; it does not result in positive behavior change; it tears apart, rather than unites, the team. Ban it!

That does not mean one member of a team cannot serve as a sounding board for another member in need of advice about a third team member. But, in doing so, the aim must be to enlist a sympathetic ear and seek counsel, rather than to recruit additional muscle to further a pet cause.

A corollary rule relates to the sounding board. He or she must hold the individual seeking advice accountable for either dealing directly with the conflict or letting it go. Furthermore, the person seeking advice must report back to the sounding board about how the issue was resolved.

Some senior teams have developed strict procedures relating to third-party involvement. At Arnott's Biscuits Limited, Campbell's largest Asia-Pacific division, president John Doumani and his senior team devised the following protocols for escalating conflict:

❐ Individual issues will be raised from member to member for resolution.

❐ If there is no resolution, the members involved can choose (together) an appropriate third-party mediator. The first person they should consider is the team's facilitator.

❐ If no resolution, the issue is to be escalated to the team mentor, who may advise or be a source of input to aid in the decision.

❐ Team members have the right to escalate an issue decision to the full team. The mentor should assist the team as necessary prior to escalation.

Whether it falls to the team leader, the team facilitator, or the full team to resolve intrateam disputes, it behooves the team to act quickly, which leads us to another important protocol.

❐ *Resolve it or let it go.* The longer conflict remains unresolved, the greater the chance that it will metastasize, spreading its poison throughout the team. To cut off conflict before it spreads, some teams adhere to a deadline of twenty-four or forty-eight hours for conflict resolution.

When two members of a team have an issue between them, the team leader gives them a deadline to resolve it. If, at the end of that time, they have not been able to do so, they are expected to drop the issue completely and move on.

❐ *Don't accuse in absentia.* Even an accused felon has a right to hear the charges against him and to defend himself in open court. So should every member of the senior team. If, during a team meeting, someone brings up an issue that involves another member who is not in attendance, the discussion should stop immediately. The team owes it to that person to postpone further debate until the absent person can be heard from.

❐ *Don't personalize issues.* John Stuart Mill once observed that the key to progress is to let all ideas start off even in the race. Eventually, the truth will prevail. In business settings, differences of opinion and viewpoints have a way of stimulating new ideas and strengthening outcomes, provided the discussion can be depersonalized.

One booby trap to avoid might be called the genetic fallacy, which assumes that an issue stems from the inherent animosity of the person or group expressing it. The president of one mid-size financial institution had a vice president of sales on his top team who felt that anyone who interrupted him during a meeting was, in effect, telling him to "shut up." Often, the interruption was merely an attempt by another person to open up the discussion. Even after the team worked out a signal to politely interrupt the talkative executive, he continued to feel slighted. Eventually, he left for less intrusive pastures.

A senior executive who has been far more successful in depersonalizing conflict is Campbell Soup's John Doumani. Of depersonalization, Doumani says that:

> What it means to me personally is that the issues that we are dealing with are all about the job; they should be dealt with in the context of the job. So if people have an issue with me about the way I do my job, that's not an issue with me as a person. It doesn't strike at the core of who I am. It's feedback about the way I do my job, so I don't take it personally.

It is important to learn, both when giving and receiving feedback, how to maintain a depersonalized position. On the side of the person who is providing the feedback, whether to a direct report in an annual performance review or to a peer in a team meeting, this means stating your concerns in terms of observable behaviors, not feelings. Instead of using formulations such as, "I'm disappointed in your performance," or

"You've got to improve your attitude," stay focused on specific behaviors that the person can focus on improving. Stating that "Your department's productivity dropped 7 percent this quarter," or "I have called you three times to set up a meeting, and you haven't returned my calls," is likely to be met with less defensiveness and result in more positive action.

If you are the recipient of feedback from your boss, your peers, or your direct reports, try to follow John Doumani's example: Remember that it is about the way you are doing your job, not your worth as a human being. And remember that it works both ways: If you feel that they are not stating their concerns in a depersonalized fashion, ask them for more objective measures of your performance and for behavioral evidence related to those measures.

Depersonalizing is not easy. In fact, learning to look at a workplace issue as a business case is one of the hardest things that executives must do. But it often brings big payoffs. Peter Wentworth, vice president of global human resources for Pfizer's consumer health care division, believes that the ability to depersonalize conflict goes hand in glove with the ability to come up with creative solutions to business problems.

Wentworth believes that one of the positive byproducts of conflict is that you have the opportunity to hear everyone's side of the story, to look at the same situation from several different perspectives, and, after all the points of view have been expressed, to make a more informed decision—but only if you can depersonalize.

If, on the other hand, you persist in interpreting other people's suggestions as threats to your position or attempts to expand their territory at your expense, you will never reap the benefits that come from adopting an unbiased viewpoint.

❐ *No hands from the grave.* Lee Chaden is senior vice president of human resources for the Sara Lee Corporation. Before assuming this position in August 2001, he ran the corporation's collection of eight or nine European apparel companies, a $2 billion business headquartered in Paris.

Each of these companies was actually a freestanding business that often competed with the others in the marketplace. In his early days as leader of this group, Chaden recalls that he would walk out of a meeting with the leaders of the companies believing that resolution on which styles each one would offer in a given country had been reached, only to receive a frantic telephone call from one of them a few days later accusing another person of violating the agreement.

As soon as Chaden became aware of the delayed disagreements and second-guessing, he asked his executive committee to establish a no-hands-from-the-grave protocol. For example, one contentious issue facing Chaden and his team related to some of the Sara Lee companies wanting to copy designs from one another to sell to private-label customers. Chaden might argue that such copying should not be allowed until six months after a product launch, since that is about the time it would take the competition to copy the styles. The private-label advocate, on the other hand, might argue that it takes less time than that, and so on.

The executive committee did not leave the room until a firm agreement had been reached on the issue and recorded in meeting minutes. There was to be no second-guessing and no *ex post facto* finessing—in other words, there would be no hands from the grave.

Another strong proponent of the no-hands-from-the-grave protocol is Manuel Jessup, vice president of Sara Lee Underwear, Sara Lee Socks, and Latin America North for Sara Lee Corporation. Referring back to his hypothetical example of deciding to freeze salaries even though many senior-team members disagreed, he added, "Some people may walk out of the room and continue to complain about what we did. They want us to go back and revisit our decision. To them I say, 'The train has left the station, and it's not coming back.'"

Protocols Beyond the Team

In the manner in which members of the senior team are constantly interacting with one another, they are also in constant contact with the functions they represent. Many of the issues that arise in their meetings cannot be resolved without the input of people in their function—that is, sales problems require the expertise of national and regional sales directors; those who conduct market research need to be consulted before major marketing decisions can be made, and so forth. How is this information to be captured and conveyed to the senior team? How will functions not represented on the team make their voice heard? Protocols are needed to handle these and other extra-team issues.

In this area as well as that of team-based protocols, Arnott Biscuits has developed a set of clear, specific protocols:

Beyond the Team

- ❒ The team's functional representative manages the issue back to the function for decision, clarification, information, or advice.
- ❒ The team mentor might assist with the resolution of team versus function issues. The process for resolving these issues will be carried out according to the internal team protocols.
- ❒ The functional representative responds to the team on issues with any supporting evidence/expertise.
- ❒ The team facilitator ensures that issues from those functions that are not represented on the team are raised to the team.

Communication Protocols

Once the senior team has embarked on the conflict-management journey, a number of decisions relating to the rest of the company need to be made. Most senior-team alignments take place off-site, and when the team members return to the workplace, their direct reports often have questions about what they have been doing. How much information about the team's alignment efforts should be shared? Who should share it? When, and in what form? Before going back to the so-called real world, the team needs to develop protocols—a party line, as it were—to govern its communications with the rest of the organization.

A Final Word on Protocols

Protocols must be embedded into a company's view of "how business is done around here." To ensure that the team continues to subscribe to its protocols, make certain they are written down and circulated. Keep them posted in the room where the senior team meets. And revisit them periodically, as a group, to assess whether or not they are being observed and if additional protocols are needed to support the team in its conflict-management efforts.

Business Relationships/Mutual Expectations

How well a team works to align its goals, roles, and protocols speaks volumes about the interpersonal relationships among its members, which is the fourth key element that must be aligned within senior teams. These relationships are often the holding pen of conflict. In dysfunctional teams and organizations, it is where silo thinking and subterfuge surface.

In Chapter 1, we discussed the roots of conflict: the deep-seated beliefs that have been ingrained over a lifetime, the resulting core-limiting beliefs and going-in stories that predispose people to certain behaviors, and the range of communication styles that characterize employee interactions. We outlined the three basic styles on the behavioral continuum: nonassertive, assertive, and aggressive. To recap:

❐ The nonassertive individual, in effect, says, "I've got needs and so do you, but I'm not telling you what mine are. And if you don't guess them, I'm going to hold it against you." The nonassertive individual is Mount Saint Helens waiting to erupt.

❐ At the other extreme, the aggressive individual proceeds on the basis that "I've got needs and, at best, so do you, but mine count more." This is the schoolyard bully in business attire.

❐ In the middle are assertive individuals, who recognize that both parties in a conflict situation have needs and strive for a negotiated settlement. This is the effective conflict manager.

Each behavior on the continuum has payoffs, and each exacts a price. For the nonassertive executive, the payoff is avoiding arguments and coming across as a team player. But the price is steep in terms of unmet needs and diluted effectiveness.

Aggressive executives often get their way and benefit from the charisma of machismo. They pay the price, however, in alienating others, closing down input and feedback, and failing to gain commitment, especially in the new knowledge-based organization.

Although being assertive forces compromise and takes patience and time, it has all the benefits of a win-win approach.

Training in conflict resolution involves understanding the payoffs and price of each behavior on the continuum; demarcating the boundaries of nonassertive, assertive, and aggressive behavior; and learning how to avoid crossing into the extremes. Knowing oneself is the first step in the process.

Eliminating Blind Spots

"Know thyself" is a time-honored injunction. Conflict management situations require achieving a balance between knowing yourself and deciding what and how much to reveal to other people. The Johari Window[2] depicted in Figure 2-4 is a graphic representation of the various ways in which we share information about ourselves with the outside world.

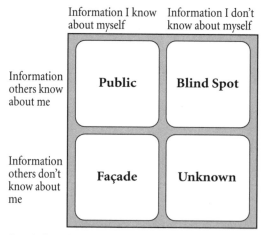

Source: Jones and J. Pfeiffer, editors, *The 1973 Annual Handbook for Group Facilitators* (New York: Pfeiffer & Co., 1973). Copyright © John Wiley & Sons, Inc. This material is used by permission of John Wiley & Sons, Inc.

Figure 2-4. The Johari window.

While we are not advising showing home movies of your soul to colleagues, the more information about ourselves we share with others—the more of an "open book" we strive to be—the less likely that we will find ourselves in conflict with others. When we choose to keep our thoughts, beliefs, and feelings hidden, we sow the seeds of conflict. By maintaining a false façade, we set ourselves up to be misunderstood. Similarly, when we avoid looking at ourselves objectively, the blind spots that we develop become a breeding ground for disagreements.

One of the biggest challenges we face in life is, as Robert Burns described it, "to see ourselves as others see us." It takes a great deal of skill—and courage—to look at ourselves through the eyes of others. It takes even more of both to modify our behavior based on the feedback they give us. If we are serious about resolving the conflict that hinders us, however, it behooves us to eliminate our blind spots, particularly those that relate to our communication style.

We can only get a true picture of the way we interact with others by being open to their feedback—by soliciting from them the information they have and we do not. This is what sociologist W.I. Cooley calls "the looking-glass self." It is the reason that the exercise that we described in Chapter 1—where each person assesses his or her style, then other team members offer their opinions—is so useful.

Remember Dan, the executive who saw himself as assertive but not aggressive? Feedback from his fellow team members made Dan aware of a large blind spot in his assessment of himself. With this new knowledge about himself, Dan began to realize why the air often became thick when he entered a room and why many of his colleagues went on the defensive as soon as he began talking.

The next step was for Dan to begin moderating his behavior—changing his position on the continuum. He made a contract with the female executive who had revealed exactly how intimidating she found him, promising to be less aggressive during their interactions. She, in turn, promised to speak up when she felt intimidated rather than keeping her feelings pent-up and allowing her resentment to fester.

The ultimate goal when it comes to business relationships is for everyone on the team to be assertive. People who are nonassertive, for example, must learn how to protect their boundaries and express their agenda without crossing the line into aggression. The aggressive individual, by contrast, must learn not to violate the boundaries of other people. Chapter 5 will address the skills executives can cultivate to facilitate their move along the continuum.

From Alignment to Action

Aligning a team in the four key areas goes well beyond capturing ideas on an easel, getting everyone around the table to nod in agreement, and then sitting back and waiting for behavior to change. There must be serious commitment to action and a willingness on the leader's part to hold colleagues accountable for honoring the contracts they have made.

When Chuck Nesbit assumed the top position at Bali Company, now Sara Lee Intimate Apparel, he knew that getting his management team to become less fragmented and more interdependent would require a serious commitment on everyone's part. He began by working with his senior team to clarify goals and roles and to establish the necessary protocols. As part of the team-development process, each member was sent off with a colleague to discuss disconnects in the working relationships, agree on a possible solution, and develop action plans. The focus was on priority issues and the future—on what could be changed—rather than on reliving the past.

The agreements or contracts forged between each pair of executives were discussed with the entire senior team so everyone became accountable for success. Part of the contracting process involved encouraging the team to commit to a set of ground rules, similar to the ones already described, for dealing with conflicts that may arise during the issue-resolution process. These rules are periodically assessed and updated by the senior team to ensure their ongoing viability and to discuss the lessons learned.

As a result of this process, Nesbit's team began to function like owners of a company. Executives were given carte blanche to discuss problems that surfaced in one another's areas. Silos crumbled. Traditional rivalries gave way to a focus on what was best for the business. And, best of all, Nesbit extricated himself from the triangulation trap, which freed him to focus on issues of more strategic importance.

Teams like Nesbit's, which have achieved alignment in all four areas of the pyramid, are on their way to achieving high performance. Chapter 3 will explore the other attributes of high-performance teams and how to achieve them.

Notes

1. Based on the work of Robert L. Katz. For further details, see Robert L. Katz, "Skills of an Effective Team Leader," *Harvard Business Review,* September 1974, pp. 90–102.
2. "The Johari Window: A Model for Soliciting and Giving Feedback," *The 1973 Annual Handbook for Group Facilitators*, University Associates, 1973, pp. 114–120.

CHAPTER 3

High-Performance Teams and Conflict Management

*"Today, more than ever, success depends on hav-
ing the ability to communicate and execute a consistent, unified vision across product, advertising,
sales, packaging, etc.—and that requires a team
that to the consumer appears as one."*

—Lew Frankfort, chairman and CEO, Coach

When word of the World Trade Center attacks hit the
street on September 11, 2001, New Yorkers rushed to
the aid of those who had been trapped in the towering infernos.
Having no idea that the majority of the victims had been killed
outright and anticipating that a large number of injured people
would need blood, they rushed to local hospitals and blood
centers to donate the gift of life. Americans throughout the nation quickly followed suit.

Soon, what had begun as a response to the disaster became
a crisis in itself. All the blood that was donated needed to be

tested before it could be processed and stored for later use. And the tests needed to be carried out within a week of donation, or the blood would need to be discarded.

Only two U.S. companies, Abbott Laboratories and Johnson & Johnson's Ortho Clinical Diagnostics, Inc. (OCD), manufacture the instruments and software that are used to test donated blood for hepatitis, human immunodeficiency virus (HIV), and other infectious diseases. On September 11, the amount of product that the two companies had shipped to blood collection centers and kept in inventory had been based on forecasts made months before the tragedy—and was only between one-quarter and one-third of what was suddenly needed. At both companies, manufacturing, quality control, regulatory testing (materials must pass inspection by the FDA before they can be shipped), and distribution all needed to be ratcheted up instantly to meet the unexpected demand.

Cathy Burzik is president of Ortho Clinical Diagnostics, Inc. Reporting to Burzik is a board composed of OCD's functional vice presidents. Tony Zezzo is vice president and general manager of sales and marketing for OCD operations in the United States. On September 11, Burzik was in Japan, so it fell to the OCD board to come up with a solution to the crisis.

High Performers to the Rescue

Four hours after the towers' collapse, the board had met and formed a crisis team made up of the organization's functional heads. The team identified the internal constraints to replenishing inventories and quickly developed a plan to overcome each. The first step was to establish communication with the key players in operations, the field, and the competition.

Members of the team contacted their counterparts at Abbott Labs to explore ways in which the two companies might be able to save precious resources by coordinating their efforts and providing assistance to one another. At the same time, OCD's field organization was pressed into twenty-four-hour service, making calls to determine exactly how much inventory blood centers had at their disposal. Other members of the team began working with the FDA to streamline the process by which product is inspected and released.

Simultaneously, the manufacturing department inventoried the raw materials it had in stock and identified which additional materials, and how much of each, were needed. Non-blood-testing product lines were shut down; their finished products were shipped or stored to make room for blood-testing products; and the lines began churning out blood-testing products.

The biggest challenge facing OCD was distribution. Blood-testing products carry an expiration date and are, therefore, always shipped by air. But all commercial flights remained grounded in the days following the attack. A call was made to Johnson & Johnson's executive committee, which immediately approved the use of the company's corporate fleet to deliver the much-needed testing supplies. The plan was presented to the Federal Aviation Association (FAA), which immediately obtained clearance for the fleet to fly with "lifeguard status" throughout the country. Within twenty-four hours, Johnson & Johnson jets were shipping product to locations that had the greatest need for the testing materials. OCD employees remained on duty twenty-four hours a day, seven days a week, and product flowed continuously to the blood centers, until the crisis was over.

As this example demonstrates, Johnson & Johnson has empowered its employees to solve problems and make decisions without having to go back up the chain of command for approval at every step. Johnson & Johnson's long-standing decentralized management system stands in stark contrast to the hierarchical structure that until recently characterized most businesses.

The Way We Were

The traditional business organization evolved over many years. German sociologist Max Weber observed that the Industrial Revolution put a premium on the specialization of labor. Organization form and structure followed the need. What emerged were hierarchically structured entities in which workers at the lowest level reported to first-line supervisors who, in turn, reported to middle managers in their function.

Middle management, which typically consisted of several layers within a function, was organized the same way, with each ensuing level possessing more decision-making responsibility and authority than the one beneath it.

The highest level of middle management reported to the top manager of the function—usually a senior vice president—who, in turn, reported to the president or CEO. This individual, with or without the input of his vice presidents, made strategic decisions and sent them back down through the hierarchy to be implemented.

In this model, the various functions that made up the organization remained separate—or kept in silos—all the way to the top. Key operational decisions related to each function were made by the senior vice president of that function, who, mirroring the CEO, made the decisions and relied on his underlings to implement them. As in the military, to which it bore more than a passing resemblance, "command and control" was the paradigm of the hierarchical organization.

For most of the century and a half following the Industrial Revolution, the hierarchical organization flourished, in large part, because of the high degree of control its leaders were able to exercise. Henry Ford, Alfred Sloan, Andrew Carnegie, Thomas Watson, John D. Rockefeller, William Randolph Hearst, and other giants of modern-day business built empires by running a tight ship—that is, retaining near-absolute power over the vast hierarchical organizations they had created.

In the last half of the twentieth century, however, the traditional business organization fell under attack by the four horseman of the revolution around us: globalization, the growth of information technology, new forms and intensity of competition, and pressure for rapid innovation.

The Changing Face of Organizations

Sustainable competitive advantage is a terrific goal, but you can no longer count on it. Not long ago, companies could rely on their products, relationships with customers, technology, and natural and financial resources to provide at least some period of homeostasis before the next round of disruption and change.

No more. Product life cycles have shortened, while the pace of technological invention and advance has quickened. Advancements such as cell phones, computers, Internet access, broadband, just-in-time inventory systems, robotics, mass customization, and genomics have cleared away the entrenched competitive advantage of companies not nimble enough to adapt to changing times.

The need for a high-speed, "intelligent" enterprise has made obsolete the hierarchical organization, with its multiple layers, slow-motion decision making, and dependence on the personality of the leader. Today's most successful business organizations are characterized by fewer levels and decentralized decision points. In these companies, command and control from the top have given way to consultation and collaboration throughout. Silos have toppled, replaced by cross-functional problem-solving, decision-making, and planning teams.

Figure 3-1 contrasts the distinguishing characteristics of the once-predominant hierarchical organization with those of today's horizontal one.

The Need for Speed

Bill Gates exhorts companies to do *"Business @ the Speed of Thought."* Strategy guru Adrian Slywotsky believes in the law of

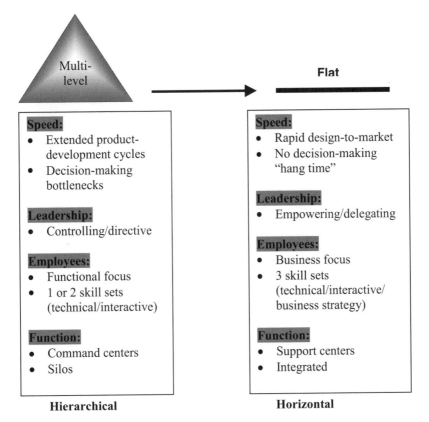

Figure 3-1. Hierarchical vs. horizontal organizations.

"survival of the fastest." The National Aeronautics and Space Administration's (NASA) Jet Propulsion Lab practices high-velocity leadership. Companies are striving to do business in real time, with the shortest possible lapse between idea and action, initiation and result. The authors of *Culture.com* say that business in the New Economy is transacted ten times faster than before: Changes that once took ten years to make now happen in one year. To succeed, they say, businesses must "make the jump to warp speed."[1] Which is why, among the differences between hierarchical and horizontal organizations that are listed in Figure 3-1, that of speed is probably the most critical.

Top executives do not move to the horizontal organization as a result of a sudden awakening or Pentecostal experience. Sadly, there are no tongues of fire descending on the uninitiated top team, with everyone suddenly proclaiming, "Let's go horizontal" or "We gotta have high-performance teams."

More typically, a company contemplates a major strategic shift or is confronted by a significant business issue. Perhaps the new strategy calls for breaking out of the current product configuration, or it requires the company to enter new, unfamiliar markets. Maybe the company's technology base must be recast, or perhaps it merely needs to put more oomph behind its brands or customer groups.

In other words, a challenge presents itself—one that interrupts the traditional management rhythms. Members of the senior team begin to realize that the playing field is changing. The old star-chamber approach, where executives at the top make the key calls, is becoming passé. It is too slow and does not harness the brainpower and drive of others in the organization, especially those who interact with customers.

Smashing Silos

As organizations have shifted from the hierarchical to the horizontal model, management gurus have rushed to fill the vacuum. To wit: empowerment, reengineering, self-directed teams, knowledge management, the learning organization—we have hardly scratched the surface! These and many other initiatives have been touted as the best way to achieve maximum energy and speed and, therefore, competitive advantage.

Here is the baseline point that can easily be missed in all the hubbub: *The one competitive advantage that cannot be easily bought, imitated, or made obsolete is superior management of people and processes, including those that deal with conflict management.* The best way for an organization to achieve this advantage is by creating and nurturing high-performance teams from the top down.

High-performance teams are in effect pools of synergy, designed to leverage talent by bringing together diverse viewpoints, experiences, judgments, and capabilities, along with essential information needed to resolve business issues. Diversity can open the floodgates of dysfunctional conflict, but not in high-performance teams, where open and direct conflict is characterized by the dynamic tension discussed in Chapter 1.

High-performance teams subvert traditional hierarchical organizations. The old top-down model, with its silo thinking, is swept away. Employees are asked, often for the first time, to assume individual and collective responsibility for business results. In effect, high-performance teams become mini boards of directors. The compass points of team members are more oriented to the customer than to their bosses and more toward "we" than toward "my function."

The senior management team should be the ultimate high-performance team in an organization. Even in the old hierarchical model, the CEO and his or her key lieutenants made up the one team that, at least on paper, was constituted to work cross-functionally. In horizontal organizations, cross-functional teams are empowered at many junctures.

We have worked with cross-functional brand and product teams, market teams, customer teams, product-development teams—and the list goes on. Masterfoods USA, for example, makes several brands of candy, including M&Ms and Snickers, as well as Uncle Ben's Rice and Pedigree, Whiskas, and Sheba pet foods. To support the company's product-focused strategy and brand structure, senior management has set up brand teams. Each team is responsible for solving problems and making decisions related to its particular brand. In contrast, the New Zealand Dairy Board, which is also product-focused, sells all its products under one brand name. Each of its cross-functional teams represents a single product line—milk, cheese, butter, or yogurt—within that brand. On the other hand, Sara Lee Intimate Apparel, which sells numerous products to Wal-Mart, K-Mart, and other giant retailers, has organized into customer-business teams in accord with its customer-centric strategy.

In each of these organizations, the business teams are made up of key players from every functional area that has a stake in the process or operation under consideration. It is the senior-management team's responsibility to decide which functions will be represented on a team. But no matter who sits on a team, they are all expected to work together and become accountable for high performance.

It Doesn't Stop at the Top

High-performance teams begin at the top. When the senior management team senses a gap between the "should be" and the "as is," its first task is to ask itself, "How can we move to new levels of performance?" The answer to that question should be: "You need to become aligned in the four areas of the pyramid: goals/business priorities/focus, individual roles/accountability, protocols/rules of engagement, and business relationships/mutual expectations." This alignment enables the senior team to speak with one voice to those outside and to manage conflict within itself.

In the alignment process, the top executive plays a pivotal role. For example, when Lew Frankfort, CEO and chairman of Coach, saw that his company's sales were beginning to slow in the mid-1990s, he realized that a major overhaul of the company was required. Determined to broaden and modernize his product line, Frankfort made the decision to transform his existing senior team, which he did not believe was up to the challenge. He created a new position, executive creative director, and he replaced several other team members who did not have the skill set required to move the company ahead.

Once Frankfort had the new players on board, they went through an alignment to get them functioning as a high-performance team that could quickly and completely translate his vision into reality. It worked. Coach made the transition from a manufacturing to a marketing company—four years ago it made 80 percent of the accessories it sold; today it makes only 10 percent—and in the process jettisoned its stodgy image. Sales went back up; the company went public; and Coach entered a new era of prosperity.

The high-performance senior-management team is the energizing principle for an organization as it moves toward becoming a more potent competitive force. But not even a perfectly aligned senior team, made of up Goliaths who excel at managing conflict, can deliver results when teams of Davids on whom they depend are riddled with strife. Aligning itself is merely the first step a senior team must take to achieve excellence.

In organizations committed to leveraging their human resources to achieve increasingly demanding levels of performance at every level, high-performance teams do the heavy lifting on key projects. To the extent that high-performance teams permeate the work environment, an organization will likely remain a strong competitive force over the long haul. Chapter 4 discusses in detail how the transformation to high-performance teams can be accomplished.

The platform teams pioneered by Chrysler Corporation in the 1980s are an excellent example of cascading high-performance teams. Created to do away with the compartmentalized engineering group that worked in a vacuum, the platform teams brought together all the departments involved in the development of a new vehicle, such as design, engineering, manufacturing, and sales. Robert Lutz, who, along with François Castaing, created these breakthrough teams, describes their power in his book, *Guts: The Seven Laws of Business That Made Chrysler the World's Hottest Car Company*:

> Before long, the chimneys that once characterized the company had started to metamorphose . . . Where Chrysler had once been highly compartmentalized and focused mainly on functions, the whole company was now moving toward a cross-functional "platform" setup—centered, not around individual disciplines, but around our major product types: the small-car team, the large-car team, the minivan team, the Jeep team, the (pickup) truck team. The focus was *holistic* (bye-bye suboptimization!), and the information flows were *concurrent* and *two-way* (bye-bye re-do loops!).[2]

Of course, each member of the platform team remained a part of his or her function. The marketing person continued to work with that department to develop a marketing plan; the manufacturing representative continued to be responsible for coordinating production schedules; and the *intra*functional team that each served on needed to be as equally high-performing as the cross-functional one.

Reaching High Performance: Evolution, Not Revolution

A high-performance team is brought about not by will but by hard work. It would be wonderful if a group of individuals from different functions and with different core beliefs, perceptions, communication styles, and agendas could—from the very beginning—put aside their many differences and work together in complete harmony. Unfortunately, day-one performance miracles do not happen very often.

Figure 3-2 illustrates in somewhat idealized fashion the contrast between a dysfunctional team and its high-performance counterpart. It underscores how much hard work is needed to transition to high performance.

From the vantage of conflict management, it is typical for a newly formed team, whatever its level and whoever its members, to progress through four different stages in its evolution toward high performance. One of the pioneers of group-development theory, B.W. Tuckman, summarized the results of more than fifty studies conducted on team development into the now-familiar four-stage model shown in Figure 3-3:[3]

On the basis of our twenty years of observing the evolution of teams from the tentative first stage to the seamless fourth, we have not only expanded on Tuckman's model in our own team-development wheel, which is pictured in Figure 3-4, but we've made it relevant to the new performance environment of the horizontal organization.

To understand the obstacles a team must overcome to reach

On a dysfunctional team:	On a high-performance team:
• Members act as though they are grouped together for administrative purposes only. Individuals work independently, sometimes at odds with others.	• Members recognize their interdependence and understand that both personal and team goals are best accomplished by mutual support. Time is not wasted struggling over turf or seeking personal gain at others' expense.
• Members tend to focus on themselves because they have not been sufficiently involved in planning the team's objectives. They approach their job simply as hired hands.	• Members feel a sense of ownership for their job and team because they are committed to goals they helped establish.
• Members are told what to do rather than asked what the best approach would be. Suggestions are not encouraged.	• Members contribute to the organization's success by applying their unique talent and knowledge to team objectives.
• Members distrust the motives of colleagues because they do not understand their roles. Expressions of opinion or disagreement are considered divisive or nonsupportive.	• Members work in a climate of trust and are encouraged to openly express ideas, opinions, disagreements, and feelings. Questions are welcomed.
• Members are so cautious about what they say that real understanding is not possible. People play games and set traps to catch the unwary.	• Members practice open and honest communication. They make an effort to understand each other's point of view.
• Members may receive good training but are limited in applying it to the job by the leader or other team members.	• Members are encouraged to develop skills and apply what they learn to the job. They receive the support of the team.
• Members find themselves in conflict situations that they do not know how to resolve. The team leader may put off intervening, causing serious damage.	• Members recognize that conflict is a normal aspect of human interaction. They view it as an opportunity for new ideas and creativity. They work to resolve conflict quickly and constructively.
• Members may or may not participate in decisions affecting the team. Conformity is often more important than results. Involvement varies depending on individual choice/commitment.	• Members participate in decisions affecting the team. The team leader makes unilateral decisions infrequently and always with explanation. Positive results, not conformity, are the goal.

Figure 3-2. Dysfunctional vs. high-performance teams.

The Four Stages of Team Development	
Stage One: Forming	*Characterized by testing and dependence*
Stage Two: Storming	*Characterized by open conflict*
Stage Three: Norming	*Characterized by the development of team cohesion*
Stage Four: Performing	*Characterized by functional role relatedness*

Figure 3-3. Tuckman's four stages of team development.

stage four, let's look more closely at the behaviors that characterize teams at each stage on the wheel.

Stage One: Testing

You know you are in a stage one team by the barometric pressure in the room. The air is thick. When you enter the room, you can feel the tension before a single word is spoken. This is not surprising. In stage one, many teams are made up of individuals who are working together for the first time. As relative strangers, they come into the game wary and inhibited. They hide behind a façade, afraid to expose themselves to the judgment of the group. Their initial behavior includes testing and assessing each other to determine the level of candor that will be accepted by the team and, especially, by the team leader.[4]

When a team is made up of individuals who have a track record of dysfunctional interaction, the air in stage one may be even thicker. One executive told us recently that until we began working with her team, she had always gone into meetings thinking that people were out to get her. Like so many going-in stories, this had become a self-fulfilling prophecy, since her defensive stance rankled her teammates, although no one said

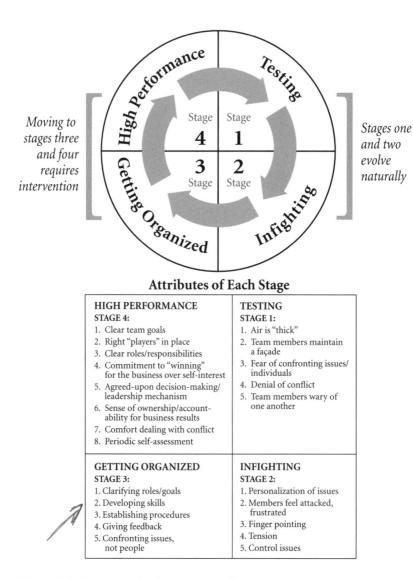

Moving to stages three and four requires intervention

Stages one and two evolve naturally

Attributes of Each Stage

HIGH PERFORMANCE	TESTING
STAGE 4:	**STAGE 1:**
1. Clear team goals	1. Air is "thick"
2. Right "players" in place	2. Team members maintain a façade
3. Clear roles/responsibilities	3. Fear of confronting issues/ individuals
4. Commitment to "winning" for the business over self-interest	4. Denial of conflict
5. Agreed-upon decision-making/ leadership mechanism	5. Team members wary of one another
6. Sense of ownership/account-ability for business results	
7. Comfort dealing with conflict	
8. Periodic self-assessment	
GETTING ORGANIZED	**INFIGHTING**
STAGE 3:	**STAGE 2:**
1. Clarifying roles/goals	1. Personalization of issues
2. Developing skills	2. Members feel attacked, frustrated
3. Establishing procedures	3. Finger pointing
4. Giving feedback	4. Tension
5. Confronting issues, not people	5. Control issues

Figure 3-4. The team-development wheel.

a word because of the team's wariness of confronting the situation.

When a team knows that candor is not acceptable to some or all of the players, many subjects remain off-limits—at least, during full-group sessions. Conflict remains underground and emerges in inappropriate places and forms, such as water-cooler and hallway conversations and ubiquitous closed-door strategizing. Triangulation is rampant, as warring parties attempt to recruit supporters. Under-the-table deal making becomes the primary *modus operandi* and is often the only way issues are resolved.

By paying careful attention to what is *not* being said during team meetings, it is often possible to pick up undercurrents that would otherwise be missed. In addition, paying attention to what is being said during meetings, who says it, and what the group's reaction tends to be can be equally revealing.

Many executive teams claim—and perhaps believe—that their working atmosphere promotes conflict resolution. But this is an illusion, especially for stage-one teams. In reality, these same teams suppress, rather than address, conflict. Team members, wary of rocking the boat of superficial togetherness, refrain from expressing their true opinions.

One facilitator was working with a project team when a relatively junior person advanced an idea that was quickly dismissed by the group. Within fifteen minutes, a vice president made virtually the same suggestion, with a slightly different twist, and for the next twenty minutes the team brainstormed ways in which to make the idea work.

When the facilitator pointed this out, the vice president was incredulous. He was not aware that the suggestion had originally came from a junior team member, much less did he realize how quickly the others had dismissed it. And he was embarrassed at the fact that everyone had bowed to his rank, rushing to agree with the idea because he had presented it.

This type of selective hearing often occurs on teams, especially when the members are accustomed to working in an organization where candid dialogue is discouraged. Differences of opinion, however well intentioned or calmly expressed, are viewed as a threat or challenge. Holding one's tongue becomes the preferred meeting behavior, and following the leader—or the most senior-level person—becomes the favorite game. It is not surprising that stage-one teams are often characterized by a certain fatalism and victim mentality.

This stage-one dynamic tends to become even more pronounced as one climbs the organization ladder. Think about it. The higher up a person goes in an organization, the less incentive there is to challenge the status quo. Keeping dissenting opinions to oneself may seem a small price to pay for holding on to a six-figure salary, stock options, a corner office, and the other accoutrements of position. This encourages playing things close to the vest, avoiding confrontation with peers, and gaining advantage indirectly, often by co-opting the CEO. Because they have so much to lose by bringing conflict out into the open, members of high-level teams often defer to the CEO.

Perhaps this dynamic explains the results of a survey that we have been conducting for the past ten years, with more than 300 executive teams from a cross-section of industries, on the subject of conflict resolution.

One of the areas the team members were asked to assess was the atmosphere in which their team works: from a wary, tentative atmosphere to one in which people are open, relaxed, and find it easy to speak their mind. Only 30 percent of the respondents gave their working atmosphere below-average marks in this area.

However, when the same individuals were asked to assess how their team handles conflict, the results were far less positive. Fifty-five percent of the respondents said that their team has little or no tolerance for confrontation, and conflicts are suppressed.

This fairly dramatic disconnect underscores the importance of "knowing thyself." Unless a stage-one team is willing to undertake the "forming"—to look at itself in the mirror and acknowledge what it sees there—it will be unable to progress to the open conflict, or "storming," that characterizes stage two.

Stage Two: Infighting

Stage-one teams most resemble married couples who give one another the silent treatment for days after an argument. Stage-two teams are more akin to the Hatfields and McCoys.

Stage two often begins after teams have been working together for a while and have fallen into a set behavioral routine. In stage two teams, viewpoints are aggressively advanced. The tension clouds that typically hang over stage-one teams have given way to thunder, lightning, and a flood of accusations. There is a great deal of finger-pointing and backbiting. Executives feel vulnerable and on the line.

In stage one, the refusal of team members to take a stand makes it difficult to gain closure; their refusal to budge from their position brings them to a similar impasse in stage two.

But stage two is not always all bad. In fact, it is here that many breakthroughs in conflict resolution take place. The fact that issues that were once swept under the rug are now being put on the table indicates that positive movement has occurred. Remember the group of German managers whom we talked about in Chapter 1? In stage one, they were afraid to express their dissatisfaction with their leader's autocratic style. When he gave them the green light to express themselves, they moved to stage two, where their pent-up anger was released and a breakthrough occurred.

But many stage-two teams are unable or unwilling to take

the leap to the next stage. They either continue their open warfare and pitched battles, or they revert to stage one, closing ranks and going underground once again.

Stages one and two are naturally occurring stages in a team's evolution. If left to their own devices, most teams would start out in stage one, move to stage two, and perhaps continue to vacillate between the two as their leaders and membership changed and new issues surfaced. But they would not likely progress further on the team-development wheel. For a team to move to stage three, there must be concerted effort and, usually, outside intervention.

Stage Three: Getting Organized

Following Tuckman's model, after the "forming" and the "storming" comes the "norming"—the identification of, and first efforts to acquire, the attributes that are essential to high performance. Stage-three teams have realized that to become high performers, they cannot continue to either bury conflict or allow it to run rampant. They must transform it into dynamic energy that produces results.

When a senior team is aligned around all four factors discussed in Chapter 2, it is on its way to high performance. The same is true for teams further down in the organization. They too need to forge strategic and key operational goals; clarify individual roles and accountability; agree upon protocols or rules of engagement, by which individuals and the team as a whole will conduct themselves; and reach an understanding regarding the communication styles to be used among and between members.

In addition, each member needs to develop key skill sets, such as the ability to influence others, the ability to listen, the ability to give feedback, and the ability to depersonalize. Chapter 5 elaborates on the importance of each of these skill sets and how to attain them.

Stage-three teams are in a learning mode. Some members of the team will grasp the needed skills faster and be more naturally adept at applying them than others. As the team progresses to stage four, its success will depend as much on its leader and these quick learners as it will on the willingness and ability of team members to follow the new group norms and processes. By role-modeling the requisite behaviors and holding their colleagues accountable for doing likewise, they can spur the group onward to its ultimate goal.

One leader who did exactly that was Joe Campinell, president of L'Oréal's consumer products division. Campinell took over the division in 1986 and led it through twelve consecutive years of double-digit growth. So, when he decided to take his senior-management team to the next stage, it was not because they were underperforming. They were doing many things properly, but Campinell believed they could do better. As he puts it:

> After going through an initial alignment, we could point almost immediately to areas in which we had made significant progress. But we felt we still had to go through a "massaging processing" before we would feel we were truly a high-functioning team. At the same time, industry dynamics kept changing, and the bar was constantly being raised. To keep up, we had to continue to evolve. We had to keep moving ahead, getting better and better at resolving cross-functional issues. And we had to start doing it early on, when the problems were minor.

Stage Four: The High-Performance Team

In stage four, "performing" replaces "norming." The team translates into action the lessons it has learned during its evolution through the team-development wheel.

Although high-performance teams come in many shapes and sizes, they all share important common characteristics. Over the years, we have identified eight key attributes that separate high-performance teams from their less-effective counterparts.

1. *The mission, goals, and business priorities of the team are clear to all team members.* For a team to operate at peak performance, its mission, goals, and business priorities must be clear to all team members. While this has always been true, it has now taken on increasing importance because of the current need for speed. As Coach's Lew Frankfort explains,

> The velocity of change has never been faster. When you need to change strategy or direction, as is so often the case today, you need to do it in a seamless, fluid manner. Otherwise, the business will suffer. Your team must stay in alignment on business goals and on the strategies and tactics needed to execute.

According to Frankfort, because of the interdependency that exists in today's complex, global organizations, the second major driver is the need for congruency. As he explains, "Today, more than ever, success depends on having the ability to communicate and execute a consistent, unified vision across product, advertising, sales, packaging, etc.—and that requires a team that to the consumer appears as one."

The process of setting team goals for the next level down

is one of diminishing senior-management involvement. At the beginning of that team's life cycle, senior management typically sets the goals. It has created the team and knows better than anyone else what outcomes are required. This only works, however, if the goals set and transmitted by senior management are clear, the results are measurable, and the team's commitment to achieve them is carefully tested. If not, senior management is setting the team up for failure.

As the new team achieves success, it assumes more ownership for achieving business results. After all, its understanding of business requirements is deeper than that of executives at the top. For example:

❏ Campbell Soup's team in Australia has a better feel for that market than the corporate team in the United States, so it sets its own priorities and goals. Senior management becomes involved in the business unit's overall strategy, but the team translates it into actual deliverables, by using SMART (specific, measurable, action-based, realistic, and time-bounded) criteria. So, a clear goal for the Australian team might be to increase the sale of chicken noodle soup in New South Wales by 20 percent by the end of the fiscal year.

❏ Kellogg's has been focusing on building up international sales to Wal-Mart. That was the overall goal that senior management transmitted to the team assigned to Wal-Mart. The team, in turn, with the input of its Wal-Mart partners, was responsible for defining specific SMART goals and priorities.

❏ Before its sale in 2001, Bristol-Myers Squibb's Clairol Herbal Essences brand was run by a cross-functional team that defined key deliverables for marketing plans, production goals, etc., for the brand.

Goliaths and Goals

Generally, the further down you go in the organization, the
more circumscribed the teams' tasks and the clearer the goals.
It is not always as simple for senior teams.

In the mid-1990s, the corporate administration division of
a large conglomerate was undergoing a raft of changes. Several
members of the division's twelve-person top team had retired
and been replaced. The reconfigured team was already in conflict. Not unexpectedly, it was in the area of resource allocation
that the disputes were hottest.

The vice presidents who made up the team represented a
variety of disparate functions, such as real estate, corporate
engineering, construction engineering, technical resources,
contributions, compensation, benefits, human resources, com-
munity and workplace programs, flight operations, quality
management, and global purchasing. Each function served different customers. Each also had its own cycle time for delivering its products and services, whether these were compensation
or benefits programs, new buildings, purchases or sales of real
estate, validations of regulatory procedure, protocols around
safety training, or the maintenance of corporate aircraft.

The member of the division's executive committee who
headed up the team had envisioned it operating as a professional basketball or hockey team—that is, as a group of players,
each of whom must know exactly what every other one is doing
at all times. In order to coordinate their plays, they need to be
totally aligned, each in the correct place at the correct time to
ensure flawless execution.

However, when the team members first met to assess their
situation, the basketball analogy made by the leader went over
like a lead balloon. The team members made it clear that they
saw themselves more as a track team comprised of sprinters,
long-distance runners, relay runners, pole vaulters, and other

individual contributors. Although the common goal of these athletes is winning points for the team, they do not need to be coordinated to do so. Likewise, each vice president believed it was up to his or her function to win as many points as possible, without worrying about being fully in sync with the others.

In truth, although all the functions were housed in corporate administration, they were not aligned by a common mission, strategy, or purpose. It was not until they began to discuss strategy in an alignment session that they realized what they had in common.

Each of the twelve functions was committed to delivering high-quality customer service, cost-effectively and on time. Each needed to help its operating companies to create value. As they began to focus on the issues that they had in common and explore ways in which to resolve them, they began to see connections and leverage points that had previously escaped their notice. This common vantage led to the articulation of an overall vision that served as a unifying principle for the division team. By focusing on common goals and working together, pooling their resources and sharing solutions, corporate administration became a winning team.

2. *The team comprises the "right" players.* High-performance teams deal with key business issues. As individuals further down in the organization begin to serve on teams, it becomes imperative that all employees—from senior executives to first-line supervisors—possess three competencies.

All team members must be technically proficient in their particular function; they must be good interpersonally and be able to reach across functions to build support to get the job done; and they must be strategically literate—that is, they understand the organization's strategy, how it relates to their function, and how it impacts their day-to-day actions.

Cross-functional teams do not occur naturally in an organization. They are not made up of people who normally work side by side. To construct such a team, senior management must make a deliberate effort to identify and bring together the key players in every area that have a stake in the process or operation under consideration.

A person can have excellent technical skills, but if he or she lacks one of the other competencies, think twice before putting that person on a team. Peter Wentworth, vice president of global human resources for Pfizer's consumer health care division, has the following advice for identifying individuals with the skills needed to serve effectively on a team:

> We look at people's track record working in matrixed organizations; we look at the impact they have had in influencing key decisions during the course of their career. We look for people who have had cross-functional roles and assignments where they really had to contribute in areas in which they were not expert, and how well they performed under those circumstances. We try to get people who don't rush to judgment, who are not overly judgmental in general, yet who have a sense of urgency and are able to bring closure to issues.

People can change. A technically competent and strategically savvy team member may initially seem hopeless when it comes to interpersonal skills. However, when provided with a few coaching sessions and a supportive team environment in which all four factors are aligned, there is a good chance the individual's behavior can be transformed.

3. *The roles and responsibilities of each player are clear to that person and to all team members.* At the former Bali Company,

now Sara Lee Intimate Apparel, as in many organizations, marketing and new product development (NPD) had a long history of competition, not only for resources such as personnel and funding but also for authority. The senior vice president of marketing and his reports honestly believed that they had the responsibility for and authority to come up with new product ideas, because of their role as custodians of customer feedback. They felt perfectly justified giving NPD a mandate such as, "You need to get this product into a deliverable within two months."

As could have been expected, the members of the development team took exception to marketing's version of the division of labor. Being the midwife of bright ideas conceived by the marketing department was not NPD's idea of a compelling vision. They did not think marketing should be mandating anything without their input, and they wanted to be brought into the decision process much sooner than the point at which marketing deigned to include them.

The two groups were stalemated, and so was the company's future product line. A company that cannot quickly bring its products to market in the trendy women's apparel industry risks becoming a dinosaur. For this reason, CEO Chuck Nesbit decided that the situation had to be addressed—and fast.

The senior vice president of marketing and his research-and-development (R&D) counterpart were each asked to write down what they perceived to be their three major responsibilities. When it became clear that both claimed responsibility for the same parts of the NPD process, Nesbit stepped in and mandated that within one week a viable process, with clear accountabilities, be agreed upon by the two departments. No longer able to remain isolated within their respective silos, the two vice presidents, along with their direct reports, sat down together for the first time and hammered out an agreement. In one week, the cobwebs were cleared away, and the NPD process was seen in a new light.

Nesbit did not stop his work at new product development. Every one of his senior VPs was asked to write down his or her perceived accountabilities, and the results were compared in the full group. Wherever unclear or gray areas were identified, the principal players were directed, as NPD and marketing had been, to bring together their respective teams and redefine the process or operation in question.

One week later, the vice presidents returned to report their decisions to the entire senior management team and to ask for approval of the newly engineered processes. In most cases, this was a mere formality, and approval was granted without question because the team knew that all the right players had been involved in the decision and, therefore, felt no need to second-guess them.

Team leaders who want to take their team to stage four should consider following Nesbit's example. In the case of a newly formed team, the accountability exercise helps to properly launch a high-performance team. Timing can be everything. In cases like Bali's, we advise the team leader to step in as soon as it becomes apparent that there is confusion in this area. Waiting only compounds the conflict and can force a retreat into the dysfunctional nature of stage one or stage two.

4. *Team members are committed to the team "winning"—achieving business goals—over their own parochial/functional self-interest.* When an individual joins a team, that person's first concern is for his or her own well-being. Then comes concern for functional colleagues.[5] Loyalty to the folks back home is fine, but it often distorts an individual's ability to commit to the primacy of team goals.

When teams reach stage three, where they begin to focus on common goals and become comfortable sharing their opinions, individual team members begin to see themselves as having a dual role in the organization. They are no longer merely a conduit between their function and the team but an active member of the team who is committed to helping the team to achieve its goals.

In stage four, team members not only recognize their dual citizenship but also know that they must put their duty as a member of the business team over their functional role. Now, the mind-set is: "I'm not the vice president of finance who sits on the senior-executive team. I'm a member of the senior-executive team who happens to be in charge of finance." This represents a fundamental shift in mind-set.

One way to ensure that team members put their common goals first is to tie their compensation to the achievement of the team's goals. At Campbell Soup's Asia/Pacific division, John Doumani and his leadership team were rewarded for the performance of the overall business, and the members of every other cross-functional team were rewarded for how well they achieved their common goals.

When their compensation is at stake, their mind and heart will follow—provided, of course, the performance environment is aligned.

5. *The decision-making/leadership mechanism that the team employs is understood and accepted by all team members.* When a team meets, there are three ways it can make decisions: unilaterally, consultatively, or by consensus. No one way is necessarily superior to another. In fact, one approach that we recommend is to work toward identifying categories of decisions and then assigning the appropriate decision style to the category. For example, the team leader can always unilaterally make decisions relating to the formation of subcommittees. Decisions that are made by the numbers might always be the responsibility of the financial representative, who is expected to

make the call after consulting with all interested parties. Decisions about team protocols might also be made by consensus. Categorizing decisions by type, wherever possible, avoids those endless debates that surface over first principles for determining how to proceed.

Setting the ground rules for decision making is a relatively straightforward process, which is tied to assigning responsibility and accountability. Manuel Jessup, vice president of Sara Lee Underwear, Sara Lee Socks, and Latin America North for Sara Lee Corporation, explains how the process works at Sara Lee Underwear:

> A decision related to the operations side of the business—for example, consolidating our distribution centers—has implications for both manufacturing and sales. It also has financial implications. So, the VPs of those functions would be consulted. But at the end of the day, as the person responsible for coming up with the most effective process for getting the product to retailers, it's the VP of operations who has to make the call.

But, adds Jessup, anyone who makes a decision, whether unilaterally, consultatively, or by consensus, has a responsibility to communicate the results, if not to the entire organization, at least to all those who will be affected by the choice they've made.

6. *Every team member feels a sense of ownership or accountability for the business results that the team is charged with achieving.* The notion of shared accountability is another important and unique aspect of high-performance teams. Cross-functional processes transcend the individual silos that exist in

an organization, and unless there is shared accountability, work can easily slip into the white space on the organizational chart. For example, the processes for moving from raw materials to end products—an organization's supply chain—is collective property. So is the development and launch of a new product. No one function or department owns these activities.

As the members of a high-performance team begin to view themselves as the custodians of these organization-wide processes, they begin to think of themselves in a new way. After all, they are being asked to operate at a level of accountability that they've never been asked for before. They must see themselves as owners of a process or operation in its entirety.

Adding to this challenge is the fact that it is difficult for peers to hold one another accountable. For example, if I'm in marketing and concerned about something going on in operations, it is my duty to question—and question deeply—the operations people on the team. At first, they might not like it, and I might not feel comfortable doing it, but any threat to the achievement of the team's goals is my responsibility. Likewise, if I see a problem between the operations person and the salesperson, I owe it to the team to see that these individuals resolve their differences. And, if I realize that it is the company president who is getting in the way of our meeting our team goals, I have equal license to say something to the president.

Pat Parenty, senior vice president and general manager of Redken, U.S.A., believes strongly in the need for team members to speak up when they feel one person's actions are compromising the team's ability to get the job done: "Someone needs to say, 'You know what, you're not cutting it.' Anyone on the team has an absolute right to say that to anyone else in front of the whole group, and there should be no personal feelings involved. It's based on how business is being handled."

This is what we mean when we say that a high-performance team works like a miniature managing board of directors. On a high-performance team, members operate as though the team's salary were coming out of their pocket. They try to bring issues to closure quickly, openly, and effectively, because every minute that conflict rages, they are losing money. In this model, each individual accepts responsibility for the overall performance of the team and, therefore, feels that he or she has license to speak on any matter concerning how the group functions.

7. *All team members are comfortable dealing with team conflict.* During stage three, team members begin, somewhat tentatively, to put issues out on the table in a nonthreatening, depersonalized way. In stage four, candor and depersonalization become second nature. Whether or not a team reaches this point depends in large part on the leader's reaction to initial outpourings from his or her disgruntled underlings.

The leader sets the tone and either helps or hinders the group as it strives to reach stage four. Those who give lip service to the need for candor and authentic interaction while taking down names of dissenters must either change behavior or stand aside in an organization that is truly committed to resolving conflict.

Susan Fullman, corporate vice president and director of customer solutions and support for Motorola, is a leader who did more than give lip service to candor. When she realized that her extremely efficient, no-nonsense style intimidated some of the members of her management team and had a chilling effect on discussion and debate, Fullman made a concerted effort to tone down her image. In individual and group meetings, she deliberately solicited feedback, both negative and positive. When they realized that she was serious about wanting their input, people became increasingly open and comfortable with her.

When team members realize that they will be applauded rather than punished for expressing their opinions honestly and constructively, they no longer hold back. They vigorously attack the dead elephant heads that have been cluttering up their work life and impeding high performance.

8. *The team periodically self-assesses its progress as a group, focusing on how it functions as a cohesive entity.* To ensure that a high-performance team maintains its edge, it must be in a continuous learning mode, acquiring and honing the numerous skill sets discussed earlier. It must also assume a self-critical role. Part of every team's standing agenda must be to look at how it operates—not only to track its progress against deliverables and goals but also how it is functioning as a team. It should ask: "How are we doing on individual accountability? On honoring contracts that we made between one another? On observing the protocols we agreed on when we first began working together?" This is one reason for writing down all protocols and agreements and keeping them in front of the team—not merely posting them on the walls but continually holding them up as standards that must be met.

Teams frequently ask how often they need to self-assess. Although there are no hard-and-fast rules, if a team meets once a week, they may want to conduct a brief self-assessment session monthly, at the end of a regularly scheduled meeting. If they meet monthly, a quarterly assessment is probably appropriate. Self-assessment should be woven into the fabric of a team's behavior rather than treated as a stand-alone event.

Even remote, global teams must self-assess periodically. They may only meet once or twice a year, but during those meetings they must ask themselves how they are doing as a group, how their protocols are holding up. Whether they meet in person, on the telephone, or by videoconference, performance against protocols must be continually tested.

High Performance Means Delivering

When it comes to high performance, actions speak louder than attributes. A team can wear itself out trying to acquire all eight attributes, but if it does not make use of them to get results, it is not a high-performance team. A true high-performance team is one that, like the one that handled Ortho Clinical Diagnostics' emergency on September 11, 2001, knows how to put to work the lessons it has learned.

Creating high-performance teams requires shifts in structure, roles, and behaviors that, for many organizations, represent major change. As difficult as this change may be, it is well worth making because, as many organizations move from a hierarchical to a horizontal way of operating, the need for high-performance teams intensifies. Only high-performance teams, with their superior ability to manage conflict, which is summarized in Figure 3-5, can move at the pace required in these new organizations.

Chapter 4 covers the process used to create high-performance teams throughout an organization.

Where Are You on the Team-Development Wheel?

Take the first step forward on the journey to high performance by answering the following self-assessment questions. At which stage is your team?

❏ What is the atmosphere like in our team?

❏ Do unresolved issues become the team "graybeards"? Is the list growing? Does anyone ever bring them up? If so, how do other team members respond?

❏ Does the group tend to avoid making decisions? Is passing the monkey a favorite team pastime? How about follow the leader?

How High-Performance Teams Manage Conflict

Each attribute of a high-performing team brings it one step closer to successful conflict management and, thus, to becoming a quick-acting, results-oriented force that is uniquely powered for success in today's global, horizontal organization:

- In the absence of conflict among team members about priorities and goals, no time is wasted going back over the same ground; no false starts or missteps, which squander precious time, are taken.

- When team members are competent in their function, there is no need to question their technical input. Trust becomes possible. The willingness to operate across functional lines also minimizes conflict; team members begin to view themselves as one cohesive unit.

- With the elimination of turf battles, one more obstacle to a homogenous team disappears.

- Once team members see the good of the team as their primary goal, they can set aside the personal and functional self-interests that often give rise to conflict.

- Replacing *ad hoc* decision making with an agreed-upon system keeps people focused, provides them with a common track for discussion and debate, and removes much of the emotional element from the process.

- Being responsible for business results gives all members of the team the same focus. Sharing accountability and ownership gives them a stake, which motivates them to work directly toward their goals.

- Being able to speak their mind freely, without fear of reprisal, and having the tools to manage conflict when it arises make team members more confident and less likely to retreat to their bunkers.

- Continual, periodic self-assessment stops destructive conflict in its tracks. As soon as the team notices the early warning signals of brewing discontent, it takes swift action to remedy the situation.

Figure 3-5. High-performance teams and conflict management.

☐ Is our decision making ruled by the tyranny of consensus?

☐ Do discussions devolve into free-for-alls?

☐ Are the airwaves monopolized by one or more highly aggressive individuals? Are less assertive—or less influential—individuals cut off when they try to voice their opinions?

☐ Are we clear about what we must achieve as a team? Do we know for certain how our performance as a team will be measured?

☐ Is the team leader the only Socrates, or do all team members have the opportunity to raise difficult questions?

☐ What is keeping the team from moving to the next stage on the team-development wheel?

Notes

1. Peg C. Neuhauser, Ray Bender, and Kirk L. Stromberg, *Culture.com: Building Corporate Culture in the Connected Workplace* (New York: John Wiley & Sons, Inc., 2000), p. 35.

2. Robert A. Lutz, *Guts: The Seven Laws of Business That Made Chrysler the World's Hottest Car Company* (New York: John Wiley & Sons, Inc., 1998), p. 40.

3. B.W. Tuckman, "Developmental Sequences in Small Groups," *Psychological Bulletin*, vol. 63, 1965, pp. 384–399.

4. A similar testing period often occurs when a team that has been working together for some time gets a new leader or new members. The injection of any unknown quantity into the mix means that acceptable behaviors will need to be renegotiated.

5. As expounded in the Gibb Model of Group Development. For further explanation of the model, see L.P. Bradford, J.R. Gibb, and K.D. Benne, eds., *T-Group Theory and Laboratory Methods in Reeducation* (New York: John Wiley & Sons, Inc., 1964), pp. 279–309.

The Road to High Performance

"Things are out in the open, processes are in place, and people—even those I once had doubts about—have stepped out of their silo and become fully cross-functional team members. . . . There's a feeling that we're moving together to conquer the next hill."

—Joe Campinell, president, L'Oréal Consumer Products Division

It's party time, and the guests stream in, sporting their best party manners. Some are happy to be there; others are somewhat apprehensive about being in a social situation; still others would prefer to be elsewhere. But everyone smiles and tells the host he looks great, although there are telltale signs that he could benefit from serious bed rest. The host shows newcomers where things are and makes the necessary introductions. Soon, guest dependency on the host gives way to socializing. Initial conversation is overly polite and wary, as new acquaintances evaluate one another: What do they do for a living? Where did they go to school? Are they single or married? How did they meet the host?

The first meeting of a cross-functional team is not much different. The team members may not be certain why they were invited and may not want to be there, but they could not refuse the invitation from their boss. They may know few, if any, of the other team members, who come from different functions, different facilities, and maybe even different countries. They too are overly polite, somewhat wary, and dependent on the host—in this case, the team leader—to get them going. This is stage one on the team-development wheel.

As the party gets into full swing, people gravitate toward like-minded guests. Some wind up in the kitchen, others in the living room, still others outside on the deck. Alcohol flows, and people begin to let down their hair. They start to voice opinions and quickly learn who agrees with them and who does not. The result is either terrific dialogue or an uncomfortable standoff. The host steps in to smooth over the differences.

By now, other partygoers have begun to form cohesive units: One group may be glued to the television set, another dancing, a third setting up the game board. When one of the television viewers walks past the dancers to get a drink, there is mild razzing: "Hey, why don't you guys get off your duff and onto the dance floor?" Most of the party has entered stage two, although the folks standing around checking their watches are still very much in stage one.

A stage-two team exhibits many of the same characteristics. Some members are stuck in stage one, either feeling that they have nothing to contribute or afraid that if they speak up they'll be put down by the others. They sit silently, waiting for the agony to end. Most of the team members, however, have begun to find kindred spirits and choose sides. Voices are raised, and barbs may be traded. At this point, many team leaders feel as though they are losing control, as though the team is being torn apart by its differences. In fact, the opposite is true: The emergence of different points of view is a sign of growth, of deepening relationships between team members. But, just as a good host needs to intervene to reduce the tension at the party, a good leader needs to manage the conflict that emerges during stage two.

At some point, the host may feel that the party has become too splintered, and it is time to get the group back on the same track. "Hey, everybody, listen up," shouts the host, and off goes the television, the dancing stops, the deck is cleared, and everyone gathers around. "It's time to sing 'Happy Birthday' to our guest of honor." It is a moment that creates a common experience and brings the party to stage three. For a while, the group is united around a common purpose. Afterward, people may go back to their individual groups, but they go back with a new perspective, a new feeling of cohesiveness.

The same transformation occurs in stage-three teams, under the guidance of a skilled team leader. By helping the team members to manage the differences that came to the surface in stage two, the leader can demonstrate that it is possible to honor one another's point of view and still come to a positive conclusion. Once its members have successfully resolved their differences, the team begins to view conflict as an opportunity rather than a problem. Having passed through the wariness and the open combat together, they feel the same sense of cohesiveness that unites the partygoers. And they too remain changed when they return to their individual groups, or functions.

Stage three is exhilarating for any group. There is definitely a feel of oneness that prevails at these moments. But how do you keep it going? How do you keep your "guests" from retreating to the previous stages? And how do you progress to stage four, where performance expectations are high and the sense of common purpose permanent?

For the partygoers, you must provide a deeper bonding experience than a group rendition of "Happy Birthday." I once attended a party where the television watchers, the game players, the dancers, and the crowd around the buffet came together not only for a few minutes but for a couple of very special hours. Two of the guests happened to be musicians, and on the spur of the moment they went out to their cars and brought in their guitars. They started playing on the patio, and before long, everyone wandered out to join in a sing-along. If parties had a stage four, this one was in it.

In stage three, the team got organized: Its members aligned themselves around individual and group goals, responsibilities, rules of engagement, and business relationships. This gave them a solid foundation on which to build future interactions. Next, they learned to voice their differences and reach agreement on how to deal with them. As with any new learning experience, success is the best reinforcer, and each time they worked through a conflict situation successfully, the stage three team became more pumped.

In stage four, all the learning has been internalized—depersonalizing conflict and dealing with it as a business issue has become second nature. Differences of opinion are no longer a major deal—they are voiced and dealt with as a matter of course. Stage four is known for breakthroughs, not only in relationships but also in the degree of innovation and productivity that the team exhibits. All the energy that was previously diverted into power struggles, animosity, triangulation, and subterfuge has now been freed up and can be channeled into achieving business results, which is what stage four teams excel at.

Creating a High-Performance Team

How, exactly, does a team land—and remain—in stage four of the team-development wheel? The best way we can think of to explain the process as it works in real life is by describing the progress of an actual team as it made its journey around the wheel. Because of the confidential nature of the data, we cannot reveal the identity of the company whose senior team, led by "Art," will serve as an example in this chapter.

Holding Up the Mirror

The metamorphosis of a team begins with holding up a mirror, helping the members take what for many is the first honest look they have ever had of themselves. This is done not by observing them and interpreting their behavior but by privately soliciting the input of each team member, then sharing the consolidated data with the full group.

Shortly before a team alignment, ask each team member to quantify, on an ascending scale of 1 to 5, the ways in which the team currently functions. This gives an anatomical rendering of the team as seen through the eyes of the members. These are the questions you should ask:

- ❐ From "not clear" to "very clear," how would you rate the clarity of team goals?
- ❐ From "not effective" to "very effective," how would you rate how effectively this team accomplishes its business goals? What would it take for you to be able to rate the team "very effective"?
- ❐ From "wary, closed, with hidden agendas" to "candid, open, relaxed, easy to speak your mind," how would you rate the working atmosphere within the team?
- ❐ From "independently" to "interdependently," how do you think team members currently work together? How

do you think team members should be working together?

❑ From "there is no tolerance for confrontation; conflicts are suppressed" to "tensions are surfaced, confronted, and resolved within the team," how do you think conflict is handled by the group?

❑ From "not clear" to "very clear," how clear are you about your role/accountability on the team? Other people's roles/accountabilities?

Then, ask team members to provide qualitative data, such as:

❑ What major obstacles prevent you from fulfilling your role on this team as effectively as possible?

❑ Describe, in one or two words, the leadership style of your team leader.

❑ What one suggestion would you give your team leader to increase his or her effectiveness in this position?

❑ What are your best *realistic* expectations for our upcoming meeting with your team?

❑ What are some of the things that are not working in the way the team functions? What is working?

The answers to these two sets of questions position the team on the team-development wheel. This exercise can send seismic shock waves through the team, and it is usually the team leader who is most surprised.

The effect is very powerful, as Gerard Kells, vice president of human resources for Johnson & Johnson's medical devices and diagnostics division, can attest:

> When the team sees the data, they realize that it's theirs: They own it; it describes them. They

realize that they all agree on the importance of
functioning well as a team, and they all agree
that they're not doing it. Sitting in the group,
having the data fed back to you, you find out
that everyone else thinks the same way you do.
But nobody has ever talked about it openly before. All of sudden, everyone's true feelings have
been let out, and there's no denying them, no
taking them back. It's sobering—and a little
frightening as well.

Looking Inward

Let's say you were one of fourteen executives on a team whose
responses have been analyzed, with the following results. What
would you think?

☐ On a 1-to-5 scale, no one rated the clarity of the team's
goals higher than 3, and eight of the fourteen rated it
lower. Comments included "no common goals have
been established for the team" and "clear from a functional perspective, but not from a team perspective."

☐ When it came to the team's effectiveness in accomplishing its business goals, once again no scores of 4 or 5 were
given. Eleven of the fourteen team members rated its effectiveness below 3. They explained, "We are still in
functional silos," "There aren't many opportunities to
work as a team," and "I work well with some, but with
others it's a struggle." To reach optimum effectiveness,
they said, they needed a unified team strategy rather than
separate functional strategies; increased trust across the

team; more opportunities for interaction; and more open, honest communication with one another.

❏ Eleven team members judged the team's atmosphere to be below 2: wary, closed, and fraught with hidden agendas. The remaining three individuals gave it a rating of 3: "People appear very polite, reluctant to confront."

❏ While the entire group said it needed to work interdependently, only one person gave the team a 4 in this area; the majority of the other members' ratings were 1 or 2. Comments referred to the fact that there was "no clear interdependence or common purpose, therefore, no reason to interact as a team," and that team members "have independent agendas based on individual business needs."

❏ Following the pattern, eleven team members said that there was no tolerance for confrontation, and conflicts were suppressed rather than dealt with. Only one person gave the team a 4 on this one. The accompanying comments reveal how strongly the team felt about this suppression: "The real issues don't get addressed; instead, we focus on superficial issues"; "Art does not like conflict, and that's partly why we don't get into it"; "There's not enough in it for me to take the risk and raise issues with the team"; "We generally deal with issues off-line."

❏ The picture was slightly less dismal when it came to roles and accountabilities, but the majority of the team still rated their clarity with regard to their individual role and the other members' roles 3 or less, saying, "The team roles have never been formally articulated" and "Our functional roles are generally clearer than our team roles."

After reviewing this data you would no doubt conclude that this team's performance was encumbered by a large amount of "space junk," as one team member put it. It is a stage-one team no one would mind competing against.

In reality, Art's team, as it was tellingly referred to— "Patton's army" might be a rough equivalent—was a group of fourteen executives who ran the sizeable North American R&D operation of a major food company. The ratings and comments we summarized are not uncommon; in fact, they are fairly representative of the data collected in initial meetings. And, although they indicate that a team has a great deal of work to do, the fact that the team "tells it like it is" shows that there is hope they will let go of the past and move ahead.

Forgetting Finger-Pointing

Art's team was too conflict-averse to allow differences of opinion to surface. Despite having worked together for several years, the team remained a collection of individuals who adhered but did not cohere. Art was the only connecting thread.

Art, of course, had played a central role in stunting the team's development. The common perception—the going-in story of the group—was that "Art does not want to hear any bad news; if we tell him the truth, there will be repercussions." What these repercussions would be, no one could say—and no one was brave enough to risk finding out. But, as so often happens in constrained, stage one environments, a myth had evolved around the leader. In reality, Art was an introvert in Darth Vader disguise. He was not comfortable opening up and sharing his thoughts. This natural reserve gave him an aura of unapproachability, although the team admitted that he was much more expressive in one-on-one situations.

How would Art need to change to become an effective leader? Here is what the team members recommended he do:

❏ Champion a vision of what is possible for the team

❏ Recognize people and their accomplishments more often

❏ Create opportunities for the group to work as a team

❏ Actively solicit and offer feedback

❏ Be open and receptive to other people's perspectives

❏ Be more candid about what he really wants

Prior to the full-group session, Art reviewed the data. At this point, he understood the importance of "depersonalizing" the frank feedback that the team had given him. He took the critique reasonably well, as do most leaders when they realize that the candid responses are intended to move the team to a new level of performance. Besides, it was difficult to argue with the *force majeure* of the team.

Art became aware of his need to change and of the fact that he was not the only one who should be responsible for turning the team around. The fact that the team was stuck in stage one was not the fault of any one individual. The group bore collective responsibility for failing to confront one another or Art, allowing conflict to fester, and not seeking opportunities to work together as a team. Everyone needed to make major changes in the way they played the game.

Depersonalizing the Data

With the field cleared of rubble, it was now time to introduce the concept of alignment to the group, using the key factors as the point of departure. Discussion centered around the fact that high-performance teams—teams that score 4s and 5s on the questionnaire—are aligned in all four key areas: goals, roles/responsibilities, protocols, and business relationships, and that such alignment is key to successfully working through conflict and attaining expected business results. The group also discussed the four stages that teams need to go through to achieve high performance. The team-development wheel was used to summarize the attributes of each stage. This exercise provided an understanding of both the dynamics of team development and an end point on which the team could train its sights.

Next, Art's team looked objectively at the data, pretending that it was merely a business case in which they had no personal stake. The team was divided into small groups, with each one considering five questions—four based on the data and the fifth on their gut feeling:

1. What are some of the adjectives that you would use to describe this team?
2. What is the main message or story that comes through about this team?
3. What are the obvious issues that this team needs to resolve?
4. Where would you place this team on the team-development wheel?
5. What will happen to this team if, five months from now, it has not changed?

The groups then reassembled to share their conclusions:

1. They had described the team as tentative, defensive, parochial, conflict-averse, frustrated, unclear, ineffective, conflicted, and avoiding real issues.
2. Several messages had been identified, including:

   ❐ The team agrees, philosophically, on the need for teamwork, but it does not know how to begin working toward that goal.

❏ It is like an all-star team that cannot agree on either the game or the game plan.

❏ It is a collection of parts waiting to be put together by someone else.

3. Critical issues facing this team had been identified as:

❏ The need to starting relying on one another/collaborating

❏ The need to trust one another more

❏ The need to enhance their listening skills

❏ A lack of shared accountability on team goals

❏ The need to improve the way they dealt with conflict, especially to make it a priority to address issues instead of allowing them to fester

❏ The need to become comfortable with candor

4. Two of the groups had placed the team in stage one of the team-development wheel; the third had placed it in stage two.

5. The groups had stated their belief that if, in five months, the team did not change:

❏ Its credibility with the rest of the organization and its ability to meet its goals would be in severe jeopardy.

❏ If the same team members remained, the status quo would continue; if the players changed, the situation would worsen.

❏ The company might consider reorganizing the R&D team, and the new model might give them less authority and autonomy.

The activities we've described are not academic exercises or sharing-and-caring hot-tub encounters. They are a tough-minded, introspective, important first step in changing the way teams think about themselves. For what is often the first time, individual team members begin thinking about the team as a cohesive social unit. They begin to see the implications of their own behavior on that of the group. They begin to realize exactly how much is at stake. And they begin to buy into the need for change.

Depersonalizing is easy to accept in theory but difficult to achieve in reality. So much of our self-definition and sense of self-worth can be shattered when others judge us negatively. During the course of an alignment, team members give one another feedback on their behavior, attitude, and style. They speak their mind and unload their baggage without sparing one another's feelings. It is not a pleasant experience. It can be tense, uncomfortable, and at times downright ugly. But it is also liberating.

Reframing Business Relationships

Whenever we have spoken about the four key factors that must be aligned, we've started at the top with the group's goals. And, in newly formed teams, this is generally where alignment begins. But in teams that have been working together in a state of dysfunction for some time, where there is a great deal of interpersonal baggage that needs to be dealt with, the sequence in which the alignment is carried out is usually reversed. Work from the bottom up: first aligning business relationships, then protocols, then responsibilities, then goals.

Depersonalizing is particularly difficult in the area of business relationships. When team members comment on the way they work together, they enter the twilight zone of communication style and the "inner person." The discomfort here is natural and, typically, short lived.

For the R&D group, the alignment of business relationships began when each member evaluated the way he or she interacted with others in terms of candor and receptivity. Ascending scales of 1 to 10 were used, with 1 meaning "not at all candid" or "not at all receptive" and 10 meaning "completely candid" or "completely receptive." One team member at a time was asked to score himself or herself on each trait, and the scores were written down on the whiteboard.

For example, Pamela, vice president of quality control, gave herself a 6 for candor and an 8 for receptivity. The other team members were then asked how their view of Pamela's candor and receptivity compared, and if it differed, why. Eight of the thirteen other team members agreed with Pamela's self-assessment. But, based on their personal experience with Pamela, three others said they felt Pamela had scored herself too high, while another two believed her self-scores were too low. Pamela then wrote down, for further reflection and follow-up, the names and comments of these five people.

After all the team members had evaluated themselves and received feedback, each one summarized for the group:

❐ Whether or not their self-perception was on the mark

❐ Where they needed to work to increase their score

❐ Who the key players were with whom they needed to have further conversation

Next, each person did additional soul-searching, telling one another how they thought their fellow team members viewed them, how they wanted to be viewed, what they personally had been doing that was keeping the team from reaching high performance, and what they would be doing differently if they were 100 percent committed to helping the team reach stage four. Then, they identified the person on the team with whom they had the greatest number of unresolved issues—the need to become more independent, resolve recurring problems, examine overlapping areas of responsibility, open lines of communication—and prioritize the rest of the team on the same basis.

It takes tremendous courage to stand up in front of your business associates and admit that you are not a paragon of virtue. But, to their credit, Art and his team did exactly that. The team's catalogue of dysfunctional behaviors included:

❐ Not sharing information

❐ Being too aloof

❐ Going underground with their complaints

❐ Listening to and commiserating with coworkers' complaints instead of encouraging them to seek resolution

❐ Triangulating: seeking support for their self-interest from Art and others

❐ Holding on to going-in stories that excused nonengagement—for example, "I haven't been here long enough. I'm considered the new kid on the block, and the team does not value my contributions."

The openness was like a spring breeze. Chapter 1 discussed the German manager whose public acknowledgment of his autocratic behavior gave his team the courage to speak up. Similarly, as Art recognized and admitted his past mistakes, his team began to feel comfortable being candid with him. One of the team members said to him, "You exhorted me not to be a part-time member of this team. I exhort you not to hold me at arm's length, not to give me just your intellectual attention, but all your energy." It was a heavy request but not an unreasonable one. Other members asked Art to:

- ❑ Include them in bigger issues
- ❑ Spend more time with them, both as a team and individually
- ❑ Discuss with them the goals of the team—tell them what, exactly, the group had been charged to do
- ❑ Let them in earlier in his thinking process so that they understand it and make a contribution
- ❑ Ask for their help and perspective
- ❑ Put their time together to better use

Art was not the only one who was asked to change his behavior. Mike, his second-in-command, was chided for micromanaging and encouraged to start delegating in order to (a) lighten the load that often made him irritable and difficult to access and (b) allow others some say in how things were run. Other team members began stating their issues and specifying the new behaviors they wanted to see going forward.

Day one of the alignment concluded with a discussion of the behavioral continuum (see Figure 1-2) and the need for team members to develop skills to move from its extremes—nonassertive and aggressive—to the center, which is assertive. The team was scheduled to attend a training session two weeks later, so at this point the discussion remained conceptual. But barriers were breaking down, and stage one was quickly becoming history for this team.

Embedding Protocols

With business relationships reframed, it was time to begin aligning protocols, or ground rules for transacting business individually and as a team. The team was divided into three work groups, each of which was charged with examining how one aspect of their interaction had been handled in the past and how it would be handled going forward. Based on an analysis of the team data, the three areas that most needed to be probed were the role of the team leader, meetings, and conflict resolution.

The following are some of the conclusions that the work groups later shared with the full team:

The Role of the Team Leader

❒ In the past Art had often been viewed as a rescuer. He had always been the main decision maker, the authority figure for the group. The others had waited for his lead or his approval before taking action. He had always been the "front man," the risk taker for the group—the one held accountable for all of R&D.

❒ In the future, Art would be less involved in day-to-day operations and more strategically focused. He would be more of a coach and mentor, a talent developer; he would be seen as a change agent for the organization; he needed to keep elevating the bar for the team. One indication that the team was beginning to take responsibility for its own destiny was that team members suggested that they needed to do a better job of facilitating decisions, that they needed to provide Art with more timely feedback and suggestions, and that they needed to tell him when they needed his help—when they felt he was too removed.

Meetings

❒ Past meetings had been unstructured, with no agenda provided beforehand and no minutes distributed after-

ward. They had been enormous time wasters; attendance
had been unpredictable; and team members had popped
in and out at will. Discussion had been guarded; information exchange had been limited, and the psychological drop-out rate had been high. After all, this was
considered to be Art's meeting. Issue resolution and follow-up had been nil.

❏ Future team meetings would no longer be solely Art's responsibility. Instead, there would be a rotating meeting
leader, and structure would replace improvisation. An
agenda would be distributed prior to the meeting, and it
would be formatted to include a business update, key issues to be resolved, progress reports on issues being
worked on, and next steps to be taken. There would be
fewer meetings, but, instead of the old sixty-minute
quickie, each would be extended to ninety minutes. Not
showing up would be the exception rather than the rule.
Forget tardiness and interrupted meetings. Open discussion and participation would become the norm. The two
team members from California and Canada would arrange their schedules to join the team in New Jersey at
least once a month. Decisions would be reached, accountabilities assigned, follow-up and follow-through
expected, and minutes distributed. The agreed-upon
changes were radical, but they were readily accepted by
all members, including Art.

Conflict Resolution

❏ Art's team could have qualified for an advanced degree
in triangulation. Disagreeing team members had routinely gone to Art, pleading their case and asking for his
support against their "persecutors." Recruiting allies had

been a weapon of choice. Accusing in absentia and post-meeting gripe sessions had become the norm.

❏ Going forward, triangulation would be out. The team announced that drawing third parties into disputes would no longer be tolerated, and each member took personal responsibility for refusing to take part in divisive practices. The team members also promised to stop behind-the-back griping. If they had an issue with another person, they would go directly to him or her and put it on the table. The use of coaches was suggested: objective parties who could help mediate disputes not by taking sides but by facilitating closure between the two parties. A forty-eight-hour rule was adopted—resolve it within that time or let it go.

Assigning Responsibilities/Accountability

During the team's reframing of business relationships, each person identified the other team members with whom they had communication issues. At this point, they thought about another set of issues—those related to responsibilities and accountability. As a team member, what issues were they concerned about? Which issues did they believe fell within their area of responsibility? In which cases were they unsure where their responsibility ended and another team member's began? Which decisions had to be made, and who should make them?

In the past, decisions had been made mainly by Art, either unilaterally or after consulting several individuals one at a time. On one hand, this practice made team members feel disenfranchised and neglected. On the other hand, it was a convenient way of avoiding responsibility and remaining uninvolved. And it increased the level of paranoia among people who felt they were in constant competition. After a decision had been made, it was usually up to Art to defend it to his superiors, a responsibility that he had willingly taken on.

Now, position became less important than value added. Who owned the information needed to make and implement the decision? Whose commitment was essential for implementation?

With this in mind, team members who had overlapping areas of responsibility set up meetings with one another to sort things out. For each issue, this involved creating a road map that outlined, in linear fashion, each step that needed to be taken to achieve resolution. Agreement was reached on who would be held accountable for each step, when they would hand off responsibility, and to which colleague the torch would be passed.

Take head count as an example: When the knotty issue of who gets additional staff and who does not comes up again, it will not be resolved by Art and the vice president of human resources. The HR executive will act as the point person, consulting with the heads of the functional and business groups. Based on the information gathered, this executive will make a recommendation to the full team. For the first time, the team—not Art—will make the call.

Clarifying Goals

The fourth area in which a team needs to be aligned to move into stage three involves goal setting. Earlier chapters provided several examples of how clear, measurable goals, which are tied to the strategy of the overall organization, enable a team to cut through the clutter and begin carrying out the job it is being paid to do. During the alignment we have been describing, the senior R&D team did not get into this area, since the top corpo-rate management team was preparing for a full-scale review of the business strategy. Ideally, the revised strategy and the opera-tional goals that flowed from it would have been in place before the teams were aligned. But, in the real world, the road to high performance does not always follow a straight line, and, on the positive side, if a team goes through an alignment prior to a strategy session, they will be able to discuss goals with a greater level of authenticity.

Moving to Stage Four

It is important to remember that, at the end of an alignment session, a team is not in stage four. To use Tuckman's verbiage, it is still "norming" and is not yet "performing." The seeds of high performance have been sown, and in the coming months, the team will probably experience some stage-four moments, but it may take months for the team to become deeply rooted in stage four. After their initial alignment, the team members must work hard to maintain the momentum, and how this is accomplished will be explored later in the chapter.

Throughout a team's journey to high performance, there are several factors that can either help or hinder it. These are highlighted in Figure 4-1.

Becoming a High-Performance Organization

Alignment does not stop with the Goliaths. The senior manage-ment team exercises tremendous influence over the organiza-tion, but it cannot proceed alone. The Davids must also turn in a stellar performance.

*There are many factors that can either inhibit or enhance a team's movement around the team-development wheel, depending on how they are handled by management. How does **your** team manage these factors?*

1. How the Team Members Are Chosen
Inhibits if they are selected because "someone has to do it, and it's your turn."
Enhances if their skills and experience are relevant to the issues that need to be resolved.

2. The History that Exists Among the Team Members
Inhibits if they have never worked together before. Has an even greater negative impact if they have a history of rivalry and ineffective interactions.
Enhances if they have worked together successfully in the past.

3. How the Team Members Are Prepared
Inhibits if the team members are not made aware of their goals, if they are not given a sense of the importance of the team's mission.
Enhances if the connection between their assignment and a strategic imperative is explained at the outset.

4. Who Explains the Team's Mission
Inhibits if it is left up to their functional leader.
Enhances if senior management demonstrates the importance of the mission by meeting with the team before it begins its duties.

5. Who Leads the Team
Inhibits if the team leader assumes everyone is on board from day one, doesn't encourage candor to get out of stage one, can't manage emerging conflict in stage two, or wants to command and control.
Enhances if the team leader recognizes which stage(s) the team members are in at the beginning, encourages candor, isn't afraid of open conflict, and is able to accept the role of facilitator rather than decision maker.

6. How the Team Will Be Judged and Compensated
Inhibits if the team members continue to be judged and compensated only on their performance of their functional duties.
Enhances if, from the outset, team members are aware that a portion of their performance rating—and compensation—will be based on the contribution they make to the team.

Figure 4-1. Inhibiting/enhancing factors in team development.

How can your organization create and maintain high-performance teams—teams that reach and remain in stage four—on every level? As shown in Figure 4-2, to attain this goal, many organizations we know pass through five major steps, or phases.

Phase One:	**Defining the Business Need**
Phase Two:	**Structuring the Teams**
Phase Three:	**Aligning the Teams**
	• *The senior management team*
	• *Business teams throughout the organization*
Phase Four:	**Moving the Message**
Phase Five:	**Maintaining the Momentum**

Figure 4-2. The five phases to becoming a high-performance organization.

Let's face it, almost every business book written by a management consultant proposes a process—usually in five to seven steps—that will help an unenlightened executive ascend some new stairway to heaven. While organizations headed toward high performance generally pass through the five phases previously outlined, this is not a rigid formula. For example, the phases do not come in neatly packaged modules; they often blend into one another or overlap. This book's aim in presenting this five-phase model is to convey the logic of the process, rather than to prescribe a lockstep solution.

Phase One: Defining the Business Need

High Performance and the Business Connection

An organization's journey to high performance begins with a business need—specifically, the need to take performance to a new level. This is not some feel-good human-relations gimmick, nor an attempt to latch onto the latest fad *du jour*. The move from stage one to stage four represents a passionate, results-driven desire to win, continually and decisively, in the marketplace.

The journey around the wheel is not necessarily a rags-to-riches story. An organization does not need to be paralyzed by internal conflict or be an underachiever to aspire to higher performance. In fact, when Joe Campinell, president of L'Oréal's consumer products division, decided to align his senior team, his operation was successful by standard financial measures, such as sales, growth, and earnings per share. The senior team worked reasonably well together, and their interactions were not characterized by in-fighting or turf wars. But Campinell realized that, as the division continued to grow, it was becoming increasingly difficult for the senior team to operate cohesively across functions. As he explains:

> In the early days of my career, silos were considered positive. But as so many activities became cross-functional, the necessity of working not as individual pieces of a business, but as a totality, became more and more obvious to us. We were in a period of double-digit growth, but I still felt that it was time to start thinking about how we could reach the next level. I didn't want to wait until sales and share growth started to slow before beginning to improve our organizational ability.

Smart executives like Joe Campinell do not wait for tough times to look for ways to improve performance.

Phase Two: Structuring the Teams

Getting Started

Jean-Paul Rigaudeau, the president of Johnson & Johnson (J&J) Germany, is another smart executive who moved his organization around the team-development wheel and, in the process, went from good to far better.

J&J Germany is the largest of several J&J companies, each of which is responsible for all J&J operations in one European country. As at L'Oréal, J&J Germany's business was healthy and growing. But, as part of J&J Europe, the issues the German company deals with transcend country boundaries. Increasingly, the German business teams must interface with their counterparts throughout Europe—and with J&J's worldwide teams—to ensure strategic compatibility and to leverage resources. And they must operate like a rapid-deployment force, providing quick and decisive responses to issues that arise in Germany and Europe. Rigaudeau believed the performance of his teams in a demanding environment could be improved by going through training in conflict resolution.

One of the first questions that Rigaudeau's team needed to think about was: "What would be the best way to structure your business teams in order to get the greatest leverage from scarce resources?" In other words, given its company strategy and the results it needed to achieve, how should the teams be organized? Around products? Brands? Markets? Specific customers?

In some companies—especially those with an unclear strategy—deciding how to structure business teams can be an agonizing process that inevitably leads to a full-scale review of the business strategy. However, this was not the case at J&J Germany. Its strategy was clear, and the three business champion teams—one organized around the skin-care business, another around the baby-products business, and the third around the feminine sanitary protection business—were already in place and reflected the product focus of the company's strategy.

Asking the Right Questions

At this point, most senior teams need to answer some basic questions about the business teams that are going to be formed, such as:

❐ How many members will be on each of the teams?

❐ Which individuals will be on the teams?

❐ Who will be the team leader of each team?

❐ What will the teams be accountable for?

❐ How will each team's success be measured?

❐ What will each team member be accountable for?

❐ How will each team member's success be measured?

❐ How will team members be rewarded for success?

In a company where new teams are being set up, getting answers to these questions usually requires a great deal of discussion before agreement is reached. These discussions generally involve the senior team and the two levels of management immediately beneath it—anywhere from thirty to sixty people—who clearly communicate objectives and ground rules and then brainstorm and evaluate alternatives. It is also a good idea to conduct focus groups with some of these players, because their input and commitment are likely to be key to the success of the effort.

Finding the Answers

In Germany, J&J teams had been operational for some time, so the senior team already knew the answers to most of these questions:

❐ Each business champion team was composed of six core members; each core member reported directly to the senior team.

❐ The members represented category management, marketing, sales, trade marketing, finance, and supply chain/ operations. These permanent members were joined periodically by other company executives on an *ad hoc* basis.

❒ The senior team had already appointed a leader for each team, who was a high-performing individual who had been given responsibility for getting the team to reach closure on open issues.

❒ The mission of each team had been clearly defined: "The role of business champion teams in Germany is to define short- and mid-term integrated consumer and customer business plans for their business."

❒ Each team was responsible for the following deliverables: the identification of strategic objectives for its category; the development of strategies for product, innovation, packaging, placement, distribution, promotion, advertising, pricing, and resource allocation.

❒ Each team's success was measured against market share, profit, and return on investment (ROI).

❒ Each individual was expected to play a dual role: functional gatekeeper to his or her function and active member of the team, committed to helping it achieve business results. As the gatekeeper, each person was expected to represent the function to the team and the team to the function. This included gathering information about the function's point of view and sharing it with the team; bringing functional expertise to the team; informing the function of the team's decisions, both as a way of sharing information with and obtaining buy-in from their colleagues; and, in the case of disagreement between the function and the team, facilitating closure between the two. The second role was far more critical: In addition to their functional responsibilities, the team members were all accountable for helping the team to achieve the business results with which senior management had charged it.

❒ The team members' individual success was measured

partly by how well they performed against their functional objectives and partly by how well they carried out their duties as a member of the team.

❐ J&J Germany already had a formula in place, by which a set percentage of each team member's compensation was tied to his or her performance on the team. In companies where new business teams are being created, a typical formula is 15 percent in the first year, 25 percent in the second, and 50 percent in the third year of the team's operation.

Once the ground rules for the J&J teams in Germany had been clearly thought through, it was time to move to Phase Three: Aligning the Teams.

Phase Three: Aligning the Teams

Cascading the Process

At this point, the focus shifted to the senior team to ensure that its goals, roles, protocols, and business relationships were consistent with high-performance requirements and congruent with the company strategy.

Jean-Paul Rigaudeau and his direct reports went through an alignment session similar to that of Art's senior R&D team. And, like Art's team, Rigaudeau's team was scheduled to go through a skill-development session within the next few weeks.

Once the senior team's alignment was complete, it was time to move to the next level—the three business champion teams that had been set up to meet J&J Germany's business needs.

Selecting Prime Movers

Each individual on a team plays a dual role: that of gatekeeper to his or her function and that of team member. The leader of the team has an even trickier, triple role: In addition to the first two obligations, he or she must assume the role of impartial observer. This entails:

- ❐ Confronting the team with candid observations of collective and individual behavior and projecting diagnoses of cause and potential consequences to the team's performance.
- ❐ Soliciting team members' input to clarify their intentions and behavior.
- ❐ Guiding the team as it makes commitments to collaborate.
- ❐ Brokering and recording contracts that define understandings and agreements about how the team will work together going forward.
- ❐ Modeling the cornerstone behaviors of effective interpersonal relationships: candid disclosure and openness to feedback.

An individual with special skills is needed to lead a team. Choosing the leader is the domain of the senior team, whose members need to carefully consider each person's qualifications and skills before appointing a team leader. Figure 4-3 summarizes the characteristics of an effective team leader. To ensure that team leaders possess all the requisite skills, we suggest that, before the teams are aligned, you provide the individuals who have been selected as leaders with formal training to hone their meeting-facilitation, issue-definition, issue-resolution, and other critical skills.

Moving the Process Down and Around

At J&J Germany, the next two days were spent aligning the three business champion teams. They went through the same

---

An Effective Team Leader:

Sets the tone:

- Encourages—and practices—candor.
- Creates an atmosphere of trust.
- Demonstrates assertive behavior.
- Displays tolerance and flexibility.
- Exhibits a willingness to change/develop.
- Treats team members with respect.
- Is fair and consistent.

Communicates:

- Gives the team the information it needs to do its job.
- Listens to feedback and asks questions.
- Criticizes constructively.
- Gives praise and recognition for success.

Is results-oriented:

- Sets goals and emphasizes them.
- Focuses on follow-up.
- Takes responsibility for getting closure on decisions.
- Facilitates the setting of protocols and holds the group to them.
- Keeps the team focused on how well it is managing conflict.

Represents the team to the organization:

- Speaks knowledgeably about the team's goals and progress.
- Demonstrates loyalty to the team.
- Advocates for the team when appropriate.

Figure 4-3. The characteristics of an effective team leader.

process as the senior team, such as gathering data prior to the session, holding up the mirror (looking at the data in full group), depersonalizing the data and describing their team as if they were outside observers, and speaking candidly about the issues they had with one another. Next came the alignment around the four key alignment factors: goals, responsibilities, protocols, and business relationships.

At the end of this alignment, the three teams focused on the level beneath them: How should teams on that level be organized, who should lead them, how should their success be judged and rewarded?

They also devoted time and thought to the message they wanted to convey about the experience they had recently gone through. What should they tell their direct reports was the goal of the two-day session? What went on? What were some of the outcomes? What differences would they be seeing in the behavior of the business teams? Before the end of the session they had to reach agreement on the amount and type of information they made public, so that the message they sent out was clear and consistent.

The process will continue, down through J&J Germany, until all its business teams are on the road to high performance. That means all cross-functional teams and all interfunctional ones as well. It is a lofty goal, but one that can be accomplished with the determination of senior management and the commitment of the organization. Achieving that commitment is the goal of Phase Four: Moving the Message.

Phase Four: Moving the Message

Opening Up the Dialogue

As with any major organizational change, the key to successfully creating high-performance teams lies in communicating the objectives and obtaining the buy-in of all employees. If you omit this step, you can forget high performance. Communication is not merely about talk, it involves explaining the transformation, testing for understanding, relating it back to everyone's job, and then answering the question: What's in it for me?

At J&J Germany, the communication process was set in motion prior to the alignment sessions, when the senior team met with the next two levels to discuss the business need and the structure of the teams. On Monday and Tuesday, the senior team was aligned; on Wednesday and Thursday, it was the turn of the three business teams. On Friday, all four teams met to share their experiences and to resolve any issues that had come up during the alignments.

The multiteam discussion centered around how much decision-making authority each team would actually have, how often the senior team wanted to meet with them to review results, and what would be the process for escalating conflict that could not be resolved within the team. The meeting served another important purpose: It reassured the teams that senior management was serious about empowering them to achieve business results.

At this point, all four teams scheduled skill-development sessions. The aim was to sharpen the teams' ability to confront issues—and one another—head-on and to manage conflict within and outside of the team. After attending a two-day skill-development workshop, they possessed the tools necessary for carrying out the agreements they made with one another during the alignment session.

J&J Germany is a work in progress. We will check back with them in a few months, but all indications show that they are well on the way to stage four.

Phase Five: Maintaining the Momentum

Keeping Promises

Practice is over; it is now game time. To move from the "norming" of stage three to the "performing" of stage four, a team must practice what it explored during the alignment session. Promises that were made must be kept, such as letting go of destructive going-in stories, being candid and encouraging candor in others, refusing to play the triangulation game, and putting allegiance to the team above functional self-interest. The contracts that were made between and among individual team members regarding business relationships and responsibilities must become working documents.

An easy way out would be to charge the team's leader with the task of monitoring the group and administering warnings, punishments, and rewards—in short, of acting as the group's conscience. This type of solution has no place in a stage-three or stage-four team. When beginning the journey around the team-development wheel, each team member made the commitment to serve as a majority of one. That is, each member would not only serve as his or own conscience and that of the team as a whole but each would also honestly and openly hold one another accountable.

The self-assessment protocol is among the most important. Although it is appropriate for the team leader to facilitate the self-assessment sessions, it is up to every team member, individually and collectively, to judge how well it is doing in keeping its promises. It is also incumbent on the team to take corrective action as soon as it realizes that a contract has been broken or a protocol ignored.

Working with a Mentor

One of the most important roles a manager plays is that of mentor. Most executives are accustomed to acting as a coach to their direct reports on an individual basis. But the notion of mentoring a team is often unfamiliar. At the risk of bureaucracy building, we recommend that each business team be assigned a mentor, or coach, from among the managers to which it reports.

The role of the team mentor is multifaceted, because it includes serving as an impartial third party to whom unresolved disputes are escalated, guiding the team through its periodic self-assessment sessions, explaining shifts in company strategy and goals, and assisting in the orientation of new team members. Perhaps most important, the mentor gives the team a feeling of being connected, reminding team members that they are not alone, that they are part of an important, organization-wide drive to excel.

Maintaining Critical Mass

Stage four is not utopia. Even within stage-four teams, some members may not have arrived. The stage-four team is only as strong as its weakest link.

The trick is to ensure that the majority of the team "gets it," so that the team experiences the maximum number of high-performance moments. Paul Michaels, regional president, America, for Masterfoods USA's Mars, Inc., explains how he has cultivated success in teams he has led over the years:

> One of the best international teams I've ever worked on had seven players. The team was an incredible well of potential and passion; however, four of them were incredibly high performers and pulled the weight of the others. It's rare that you'll experience a team with all of its members in stage four simultaneously, but when a team has a critical mass who are high performers you can still be wildly successful.

Passing the Baton

It happens even in stage-four teams. Just when a team begins to function as a mini board of directors, management decides to make changes: "You're doing so well, let's put some of you on another team that's not doing as well." Or a team member is promoted. And yet another heads for greener pastures outside the organization. When replacements for these veterans join the team, it is highly unlikely that they'll be stage-four players. If they are completely new to the group, they may be back in stage one, merely trying to figure out whether or not they want to be there. Better to walk softly and carry a big smile!

Many companies have developed protocols for bringing new team members on board and making them contributors in record time. Stryker Corporation's Howmedica Osteonics Division, which makes orthopedic implants, is organized into teams according to the replacement body part each makes, such as the hip team, the shoulder team, the knee team, and several others. Each team is headed up by a steering team of three executives, and each steering team has a support group called a "Center of Excellence," which reports to it.

Whenever a member of the steering team or the Center of Excellence leaves, his or her replacement is taken by the rest of the group to an off-site orientation session. There, the veterans explain the way the team operates, the issues it deals with, the role the new person's predecessor played, and any other information that will facilitate the integration of the new player.

Similarly, when a member of one of the business teams moves on, the team leader conducts a similar orientation session for his or her replacement.

Clairol Canada is one of many companies that maintain a history, or "bible," for every team. At Clairol, each team document contains the team's charter, protocols or ground rules, relevant operating guidelines, the brand and/or account strategy, the annual operating plan, the minutes of all team meetings, a list of the team's accomplishments, and so on. Before his or her orientation meeting with the team leader, each new addition to the team is expected to read the entire document. He or she is also expected to meet with the person who is leaving and to call each team member to review the business relationships that have been agreed on between their functions.

Finally, to maintain the momentum and keep from backsliding, the newly aligned team needs to have a variety of conflict-resolution skills at its disposal. Those skills will be the subject of Chapter 5.

How Do You Know You've Arrived?

The sirens do not sound to signal a team's arrival in stage four. How, then, does it know that it has reached its maximum potential—and is poised to continue the journey forward? L'Oréal's Joe Campinell describes his feelings now that his team has arrived:

> Whether it's in customer service, information services, manufacturing, or any other area— within L'Oréal our division is known for how well its teams work together. Things are out in the open, processes are in place, and people— even those I once had doubts about—have stepped out of their silo and become fully cross-functional team members. Especially at the end of the year, when we start thinking about people's performance, we can really point to an enormous change between now and several years ago. There's a feeling that we're moving together to conquer the next hill.

CHAPTER 5

Conflict Management as Art and Skill

*"Expecting people to resolve their differences
without giving them conflict-management skills is
like giving a computer to someone who's never
seen one before and saying, 'Have fun using this.'"*

—Pat Parenty, senior vice president and
general manager, Redken, U.S.A.

Imagine yourself in each of the following situations:

❐ At work, one of your peers says to you, "I don't see how you can call yourself a team player, you always seem to be focused on your own agenda."

❐ You've just joined a company as a department head. One of your new staff greets you by saying, "I've been here three years. I don't need you to tell me how to do my job."

❐ You are representing Revlon at a trade show. Someone you've never met before comes up to your booth and says, "I don't care what you say, I think Max Factor does a better job of marketing than Revlon."

How would you respond to these challenges? There are a number of options. You could choose to be dismissive and simply blow off your adversaries, saying to yourself: "Zelda is having a bad hair day." "No sense arguing with Frank, he's a control freak." "This person is clueless about what we really do." Alternatively, you could dig in and mount a point-by-point counteroffensive, or you could take the high road and ask them to explain their statements. A fourth option is to play the diplomat and try to mollify them, saying that they are entitled to their point of view and that you are certain that they have good reasons for believing what they do. And there are other decisions to be made. You could use the same approach with all three, or you may choose to be selective and employ different strategies, depending on whether your challenger is a peer, a direct report, or a stranger.

The way in which you handle conflict-charged situations like these says a great deal about your personal conflict-management style, the conflict-resolution skills you possess, and those you need to acquire.

Skills Training: The Need for Self-Reflection

During an alignment, team members take an objective look at how, as a team, they handle conflict. They look into the collective mirror—at the results of their self-assessment—to become aware of the dysfunctional behaviors that they have been engaging in as a group, such as going underground, triangulating, deferring to the leader, avoiding decision making, or abdicating responsibility. They then develop protocols, or ground rules, that are designed to stop dysfunctional practices in their tracks.

Becoming aligned around goals and roles are other important steps the group takes toward working, as a team, in a new way.

Much of the "fun" of conflict management begins with the discussion of business relationships. Let's face it: Concepts such as *organization* and *team* are abstract. It is easy for me to depersonalize when I am talking about my company or my department, but it is more difficult to do when I am talking about *me*. A moment of truth in conflict management occurs when the action shifts to the individual: when team members look, individually, into the mirror, then compare the way they see themselves—as nonassertive, assertive, or aggressive—with their colleagues' view of them. These actions get to the core of conflict management—the interactions that occur between individuals within the social space of organizations.

This self-assessment begins—and only begins—during the alignment session. It continues, in much greater depth, afterward.

We suggest approaching individual aspects of conflict management very strategically. First, use team alignment as a platform to resolve larger, organizational issues. Then, move on to developing individual conflict-management skills. Here, timing is everything. If you fold the skill-building portion into the team alignment, you risk team overload; if you wait too long, momentum fizzles. That is the reason that individual skill building should take place as soon as possible after the alignment session.

The following pages will focus on the specific skills each individual needs to acquire and the ways in which these skills facilitate conflict resolution.

The Primacy of Influence

In the old hierarchical organization, power ruled. In that environment, teams were an aggregation of individuals, usually from the same function, who were led by whomever occupied the pivotal power position in the chain of command. Although subordinates on the team were allowed to express themselves, they typically participated as information sources who served at the behest of the leader or decision maker.

The horizontal organization swept away a good deal of the old-order detritus of power. In the new paradigm, the one who wins is not the person with the most clout, but the one who possesses the right combination of strategic instinct and content capability, the ability to establish rapport, and the power of persuasion.

When Susan Fullman was director of distribution for United Airlines, she occupied a unique position in an organization transitioning to a horizontal structure. She was a cross-functional player in a hierarchical context. Her success hinged on her ability to influence rather than command:

> I was the only cross-functional person in the company. I had to interface with the director of just about every function: sales, reservations, pricing, marketing, operations, finance, I.T. These people weren't my subordinates; they were my peers. I didn't have any authority over them. They weren't used to having someone come into their area and start making suggestions about how they should run their business. The only way to succeed was to "sell" my vision to each director. And I couldn't do that without improving my interpersonal skills: learning to clearly articulate my ideas, depersonalize the way I made my case, develop my powers of persuasion—and, above all, learn to listen to each person and adjust my approach to address their specific concerns.

Baseline Capabilities

The exercise of power does not necessarily require social savvy, whereas the ability to influence other people clearly does. To be an effective influencer requires a keen ability both to assess where others stand vis-à-vis you and your agenda and to know your own style. These two elements constitute baseline capabilities for influencing other people in conflict-management situations.

Assessing Where Others Stand

What made Susan Fullman successful in her role at United Airlines was her ability to develop framing strategies for dealing with her colleagues. In other words, she was able to home in on a particular situation, assess each player in terms of the degree of agreement and support for the issue on the table, and then develop a strategy for winning them over.

Figure 5-1 provides a key to developing framing strategies. It depicts people in terms of two variables: the degree to which they agree with you and the amount of support they are willing to give you. Agreement is represented by the vertical axis, with 0 indicating total lack of agreement and 10 complete agreement. Support, on the horizontal axis, ranges from 0 (no support whatsoever) to 10 (total, unreserved support).

Do not attempt to bring a colleague around to your point of view unless you have a clear answer to the following two questions:

1. To what extent does the individual agree with your mission? In other words, does the person share the same

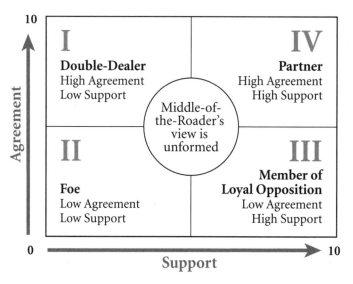

Figure 5-1. Matrix for framing strategies.

fundamental goals as you, and is he or she working toward the same end?

2. To what extent can you count on this person as a supporter?

Once you have the answers to these questions, you can begin to outline a strategy for dealing with the individual in question. The matrix for framing strategies presents the range of available options, considering the two crucial dimensions of agreement and support.

The Double-Dealers described in Quadrant I agree with you at the business-concept level but have, for some reason, decided to withhold their support. Do not waste time presenting a business case to these people: You are preaching to the converted. The key challenge here is to win their support. *Suggestion:* Focus on listening to their concerns, encouraging them to speak candidly, and working to build trust between you.

The foes in Quadrant II are the immovable forces in the work environment. They neither agree with your goals nor are they among your supporters. Influencing foes can be a Herculean task. Expect foes to be locked into going-in stories that prevent them from engaging authentically. Until you understand what beliefs are keeping them from taking an objective view, you will be unable to exercise any influence over them. *Suggestion:* Encourage candor, story sharing, and the forging of new agreements for moving ahead.

The Members of the Loyal Opposition in Quadrant III support you while disagreeing with your point of view. They trust you but are at odds with your approach to an issue. With this group, your strategy must be the polar opposite of that used with the Double-Dealers. *Suggestion:* Present a strong business case, as objectively as possible, to turn your colleagues around.

The remaining two groups—the Partners in Quadrant IV and the Middle-of-the-Roaders in the center—present opportunities. The former group supports you and agrees with you. Having them in your corner is an excellent way to demonstrate to others the value of your ideas. Partners can have a positive influence on other groups, especially the Middle-of-the-Roaders. These individuals, who have yet to form an opinion, can be transformed into strong supporters if you can identify their concerns and develop a plan to address them. *Suggestions:* Enlist the aid of Partners. Engage in candid dialogue with the Middle-of-the-Roaders, and you will likely transform them into partners.

Assessing Where *You* Stand

The second baseline capability that is key to influencing others is an understanding of how *you* deal with conflict. This entails being crystal clear on where you stand in terms of the two personality dimensions of assertiveness and cooperativeness.

Assertiveness is the extent to which a person attempts to satisfy his or her own needs. We've already gone into considerable detail about the importance of knowing where your behavior falls on the continuum from nonassertive to assertive to aggressive. *Cooperativeness* is the extent to which an individual attempts to satisfy another person's needs. When you look at these two basic dimensions of behavior in conjunction with one another and assess the degree of balance that exists between the concern for oneself and for others, it becomes possible to identify five distinct methods that people employ when dealing with conflict.

The Thomas-Kilmann Conflict Mode Instrument[1] in Figure 5-2 is a graphic representation of these five methods.

Thomas and Kilmann define each method as follows:

❏ *Competing implies being assertive and uncooperative.* An individual who chooses this method is more interested in pur-

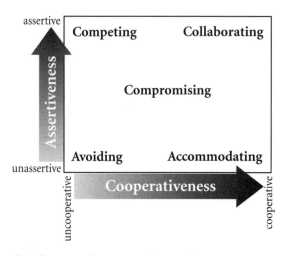

Figure 5-2. The Thomas-Kilmann conflict mode instrument.

suing his or her own concerns at the expense of others. This individual uses whatever power is necessary to win. When a person competes, he or she is defending a position at all costs.

❐ *Accommodating entails being unassertive and cooperative.* This method, which is the opposite of competing, implies self-sacrifice. The accommodating individual chooses to neglect his or her own concerns to satisfy the concerns of others. This method requires giving in to another's point of view when you prefer not to.

❐ *Avoiding is being unassertive and uncooperative.* An individual using this method merely chooses not to take action at this time, either for himself or herself or for others. As a result, the conflict is not addressed. The avoidance behavior might take the form of sidestepping the discussion of an issue, postponing it, or withdrawing from what the individual perceives to be a threatening situation.

❐ *Compromising involves being square in the middle in terms of both assertiveness and cooperativeness.* This method is often expedient. Both parties seek to quickly arrive at some middle ground by splitting the difference, in a sense. The end result might be a solution that is mutually acceptable yet only partially satisfying to each side.

❐ *Collaborating means being both assertive and cooperative.* Collaborating requires that both sides be willing to work together to find a solution that fully satisfies the concerns of each. It involves an in-depth exploration of differences to learn from each other's insights.

With these methods in mind, take a few moments to decide where on the model your workplace behavior generally falls. Then, think about the reaction this behavior provokes in others—and the effect it has on your ability to work harmoniously with them:

❒ Are you often kept in the dark because people would rather keep their opinions to themselves than deal with your hard-nosed attitude?

❒ Would your colleagues respond more positively to your suggestions if you were less aggressive and more cooperative?

❒ Are your needs frequently unmet, either because you cannot assert yourself or because you refuse to budge from your position?

❒ Do you often feel like a doormat because you would rather accommodate others than assert yourself?

❒ Do you usually seek a middle-of-the-road solution, a compromise, to put an end to dissension?

❒ Are you able to assert yourself without appearing uncooperative? In other words, are you a collaborative individual, whom everyone wants on his or her team?

The answer to the last question in the sequence separates superior conflict managers from the rest of the lot. If your answer was yes, you are indeed rare. Few people are able, without training, to cooperate without giving in, to assert themselves without stepping on toes—in short, to honor other people's needs without sacrificing their own.

The two baseline capabilities that we described are essential tools in all conflict situations. But every conflict situation in the workplace poses unique challenges and, therefore, requires situation-specific skills. Let's examine these skills in some detail.

Which Skills, When?

At the beginning of this book, conflict was defined as "the condition in which the needs or desires of two or more parties appear to be incompatible." This does not mean that resolving conflict requires the needs of each party to be met equally. All needs, after all, are not created equal or may not be equally felt. Often, one person has a need to be met or a concern to be answered, while the other has a less-pressing agenda or, initially, no agenda at all. Sometimes you will be the person with the issue. At other times, it will be a colleague who comes to you with a pressing need. In each case, different skill sets are required.

Consider three distinct conflict situations and the repertoire of skills each requires:

1. When *another person's needs* are pressing, you need *active listening skills.*[2]
2. When *your needs* are pressing, you need *assertion skills.*
3. When *both people's needs* are pressing, you need *conflict management skills.*

Let's examine the first scenario of another person coming to you and expressing a concern that needs to be resolved.

I. Using Active Listening Skills

Active listening is easier said than done. We find it difficult to listen to others for many reasons.

Studies have shown that a human being can think five times faster than he or she can speak. This simple fact accounts for much of the difficulty we have listening to others. While they are struggling to get the words out, our mind races ahead. During the lag time, we may become impatient, angry, bored, or distracted. As a result, we develop a coping strategy. We either tune them out or attempt to complete the thought for them.

Being an attentive listener is a challenge for several other reasons:

❐ *It is not natural.* The natural human response is to react from one's own sense of need. It is part of our basic survival instinct to put our own needs first, and listening to those of others is not our first priority.

❐ *Our biases influence our reactions.* Our perceptions have been molded by a lifetime of experience—both positive and negative. As a result, we have certain going-in stories about men who have long hair, women who wear miniskirts, representatives of certain ethnic groups, and people who are much older or much younger than we. These and other deep-seated biases cause us to filter speakers' messages: We hear what people say differently, depending on the preconceived notion we have of them.

❐ *We are always in our own conversation.* Because our brain works so quickly and constantly, we are always noticing and evaluating what comes into our awareness. It is as if another person were inside our head, whispering, "I like this," or "I disagree with that," or "What should we have for dinner tonight?" Sometimes our conversation with our inner person becomes so engaging that it is hard to stay focused on what a speaker is trying to convey to us.

❐ *We have a preprogrammed style.* Years of experience and learning have caused us to develop habitual ways of responding to the world around us. Add to this the impact of personality and genetics, and you find that each of us tends to react to certain situations in our own preprogrammed fashion. When confronted with another person's needs, especially if that person is in a heightened emotional state, one individual might be too embarrassed to respond, another might be offended, yet another might feel compelled to offer advice or comfort. Whatever our typical response is, it is difficult to make a conscious choice about how to behave in such a situation.

Listening constitutes one of the truly remarkable human capabilities. Do it well, and you likely will be not only an effective conflict manager but also an exceptional human being.

Nearly every act of listening confronts the listener with two divergent roads. One road facilitates the transmission of messages. Take this road and you hold the keys to the Magic Kingdom. It is this behavior that you observe when you conclude, "She really understands where I'm coming from."

The other road is filled with barriers that hamper communication between speaker and listener. Take this road and you are headed for the Haunted Forest. "Otto just doesn't get it," is the typical reaction here. In fact, Otto might as well have been wearing earplugs.

Let's begin by discussing those behaviors that set up barriers to communication. Such behaviors, unfortunately, put you on the road most traveled—and are most likely to cause ill will and dysfunctional conflict.

Listening: Behaviors to Avoid

Not focusing on those who come to us with a concern can bruise egos, but we add insult to injury by continually interrupting. Yet, many of us feel compelled to interject our own reaction or opinion into another person's story. We do this for various reasons: We are used to participating in a dialogue, not listening to a monologue; we think the speaker expects us to offer, if not a solution, at least an expression of sympathy; we want to cut short the conversation before it becomes a protracted saga. These roadblock responses cause a barrier to go up between us and the speaker.

Roadblock responses fall into the following three categories:

1. ***Sending solutions*** *impedes effective communication.* In our desire to help someone—or shortcut the conversation—we

may come in too rapidly with our own opinion. This can be discouraging to the speaker. After all, he or she may be in search of a sounding board, not a solution. It also subtly shifts the focus from the speaker and puts it on *me*.

2. *Evaluating is another way in which to alienate someone who is looking for a listener.* In our attempt to help the speaker or speed up the process, we turn him or her off by using judgmental remarks, which can signal agreement, lack of agreement, or skepticism. These remarks may provoke defensive behavior from the speaker; communication becomes tense or completely closed off; and the speaker typically leaves with a feeling of dissatisfaction and discomfort.

3. *Withdrawing is another deadly response.* When we do not have time to listen, are not interested, or are uncomfortable with the message we are hearing, we consciously or subconsciously cut ourselves off or withdraw from the conversation. We may become completely unresponsive, or we may change the subject to one that better suits us.

All of these responses block, either temporarily or permanently, the transmission of the speaker's message. They tend to lower the speaker's self-esteem, cause the speaker to become either resistant or defensive, diminish his or her sense of responsibility, convey hidden messages, and, worst of all, keep the speaker from finding a solution to a troublesome problem. Figure 5-3 is a detailed list of responses, devised by Thomas Gordon,[3] that act as roadblocks to effective listening and successful conflict resolution.

One of the exercises that team members complete during skills training is designed to mirror reality by demonstrating that, while we might think people are "there" when we are talking, they often are not. They are simply playing out their own game, rather than listening to what we are saying.

The Dirty Dozen Roadblock Responses

SENDING SOLUTIONS

1. ORDERING: Telling others what to do
2. THREATENING: Trying to control other people's actions by warning of negative consequences
3. MORALIZING: Telling people what they should do
4. ADVISING: Telling others how to solve their problems
5. LOGICAL ARGUMENTS: Attempting to convince others with facts, logic, opinions

EVALUATING

6. QUESTIONING: Searching for more information so you can solve another's problem; leading another, through questioning, to an answer you have already decided on; asking questions to satisfy your curiosity
7. JUDGING: Negatively appraising the actions or attitudes of others
8. PRAISING: Positively appraising other people, their actions, or their attitudes
9. NAME-CALLING: Stereotyping others
10. DIAGNOSING: Analyzing what others are doing or saying; letting them know you have it all figured out; playing psychiatrist

WITHDRAWING

11. REASSURING: Saying things to make other people feel better; trying to stop them from feeling as they do
12. WITHDRAWING OR DIVERTING: Pushing others' problems aside by removing yourself from them, distraction, or humor

---

Figure 5-3. Thomas Gordon's dirty dozen roadblocks to effective communication.

Assuming that your team is aligned, try this experiment at your next team meeting. Ask several people to leave the room and think about a business issue that they would like to discuss with their colleagues. While they are out, choose teams of three. Instruct one person on each team to advise, the second to reassure, and the third to ask questions—without, of course, letting on that they have been preprogrammed. When the people with the issues return, have each person meet with one of the three-member teams. Instruct the speakers to explain their issue to the team.

Afterward, the leader of the session should ask the speakers to describe their reaction to the way in which the advisors, reassurers, and questioners engaged with them. We can predict the speakers' reactions. Invariably, they will use words like "pressured," "frustrated," "annoyed," and "angry" to describe how they felt while trying to explain their issue to people with pre-programmed styles.

Team members will come away from this exercise with a better understanding of the consequences of substituting dirty dozen–type behaviors for *listening*, especially during the initial stages of an interaction.

Not all the dirty dozen responses are harmful in and of themselves. In fact, you cannot carry out a normal conversation without engaging in some of these behaviors. Their appropriateness is, however, a matter of timing. Here is a simple rule: Do not respond until you are completely certain what the other person's issue is. Interfering before that point might take the conversation in a direction never intended by the speaker and, as a result, you might never learn what the real issue is. Later, there will be a discussion of the times when some of the dirty dozen responses can have a positive effect, but first let's focus on the best way to zero in on an issue.

Active Listening: Behaviors and Techniques

Whenever a person expresses a concern or need, you, the listener, must be aware of two things: the content of the message and the emotion behind it. The content element of the message is the proverbial tip of the iceberg. The most significant part of the message is to be found below the surface—the speaker's underlying feelings about the issue at hand. When someone comes to you with an issue, you want to get past the "tip" and into the core as quickly as possible. Active listening skills are designed to help penetrate to the depths.[4]

Active listening is not limited to the ears. It involves the entire body—especially the brain. There are five effective active listening techniques that can improve your listening skills—and assure the speaker that he or she has an attentive, nonjudgmental audience:

1. *Attending Behavior.* By demonstrating attending behavior, a listener conveys the message that he or she is "all ears" and ready to focus completely on what the speaker has to say.

One suggestion, which many executives overlook, is to ensure that your conversation takes place in a suitable environment that is private, nonthreatening, without distractions, and without physical barriers between the parties. Think about it: If you entered your boss's office for a moment-of-truth meeting, what would make you more comfortable? If you were separated from him or her by a desk the size of Rhode Island or if the two of you were sitting around a coffee table?

Body language speaks volumes, as we all know, and is an important way in which a listener demonstrates attentiveness. Body position, facial expression, and gestures such as head nodding and hand movements provide cues that you are tuned in—or out.

Sheila Hopkins, vice president and general manager at Colgate-Palmolive, says that since she began to pay attention to her body language, people are much more at ease with her.

> In meetings, I had an inherent tendency to sit with my arms crossed over my chest—not exactly a body posture that says, "I'm listening openly to you." If anything, it said, "I'm listen-

ing defensively." Once I became aware of the
message posture conveys, I made a conscious effort to unfold my arms, lean forward, and adopt
a receptive, rather than, defensive posture. And
it has made a difference.

The SOLER model shown in Figure 5-4 is a quick reference
that can help listeners to remember the key points of attending
behavior.

S—Sit (or stand) squarely
O—Open posture
L—Lean forward
E—Eye contact
R—Relaxed posture/respect other

Figure 5-4. The SOLER model of attending behavior.

These nonverbal behaviors have a tremendous impact on
the effectiveness of communication. Together with tone of
voice—volume, pitch, intensity, and inflection—they are responsible for the lion's share of what people take away from
an interaction. Studies show that the message retained after an
interpersonal exchange is derived 55 percent from nonverbal
behavior, 35 percent from tone, and only 7 percent from words.

John Doumani, president-international, Campbell Soup,
can testify firsthand to the power of the physical environment—and posture:

The fundamental activity in conflict resolution
is to create an environment where people feel as
though they can give bad news and talk about
thorny issues without negative repercussions.
Once, after I'd been here only a couple of
months, our finance people were coming in to

update me on our performance. I knew we
weren't going to make our goals, and I knew
they were uncomfortable giving me the news. All
I wanted was for the truth to come out. I'm fine
when I know what the issues are; it is when I
know there are issues and no one is talking
about them that I get upset. So, I took my shoes
off and sat cross-legged on the table in my office.
When they came in, I said, "Just tell me what
you have to tell me." They immediately relaxed
and let it all out.

Sitting cross-legged on a table is not every executive's style,
but creating a private, welcoming environment and adopting a
casual, attentive style is something everyone can do to encourage candid conversation.

2. *Passive Listening.* Passive listening as an *active* listening
skill—isn't this an oxymoron? It makes perfect sense, however,
when you realize that you need to *actively listen passively.* Simply remaining silent and allowing the speaker to talk sounds
easy, but it is often a challenge, as the widespread tendency to
engage in roadblock responses demonstrates. But, as difficult as
it is to maintain, a period of silence is useful because it allows
the speaker time to express, without interruption, his or her
thought. During this time, the listener may choose to:

❒ Attend to the sender by simply listening and giving eye
contact
❒ Observe the speaker's eyes, facial expression, posture,
and gestures to receive additional insight
❒ Think about what the speaker is saying and feeling

This behavior demonstrates, without the listener needing to
verbalize, that he or she is completely involved in the needs of
the speaker.

Susan Fullman has used passive listening with excellent results in her former job at United Airlines and in her current
position as corporate vice president and director of customer
solutions and support at Motorola:

> I have a tendency to be very analytical and to
> dive right into a problem when it was presented
> to me. But I've realized that I have to allow peo-
> ple to get their act together—become clear on
> their own thinking—before responding to them.
> So, when I meet with someone I start with the
> softer side of the engagement: I try to find out
> what's going on in their head as they enter the
> room. I let them talk for some time before I even
> speak. This way, I get the whole picture, as they
> see it, and not just a little piece of what I think
> the picture is.

3. *"Say More" Responses.* "Say more" responses are phrases
that encourage the speaker to tell you more about his or her
ideas and feelings. They can be neutral statements such as,
"Really," "Uh, huh," and "Oh?" or more direct invitations to
continue, such as "Tell me more," "Go ahead," and "Would
you like to talk about it?" These responses should not communicate any of the listener's own judgments, thoughts, or feelings. Rather, the responses are meant to convey empathy—to
let the speaker know that you are putting yourself in his or her
shoes to better understand his or her sense of reality.

4. *Paraphrasing.* Paraphrasing means repeating back to the
speaker, in your own words, your understanding of what he or
she has told you. "Mirroring" is another word for this technique, which eliminates the potential for misunderstanding.

When paraphrasing, focus on the *content* of the message,

not the emotion behind it. Try to capture, as concisely as possible, exactly what the speaker has said. Then, ask the speaker to confirm that your interpretation of the message is correct.

Here are some formulations you can use when paraphrasing:

"It sounds like . . ."
"So, what you're saying is . . ."
"It seems to me that you . . ."
"Let me see if I understand you correctly . . ."
"When you say _____, do you mean _____?"

5. *Decoding and Feeding Back Feelings.* Once you understand the *what* of the message, it is time to search for the *why*. This is often difficult to do, because when people speak to one another, especially about charged issues, they often encode the message rather than letting it all hang out. The diagram in Figure 5-5 illustrates this encoding and the resultant decoding that the listener must do.[5]

The diagram shows the speaker sending—or encoding—a message to the listener. The speaker expresses what he or she wants to say, and the listener, in turn, decodes the message by

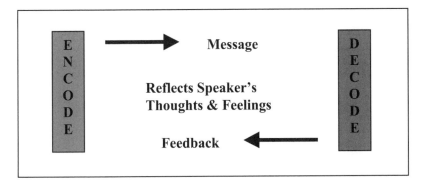

Figure 5-5. Decoding a speaker's message and feeding it back.

reflecting back the thoughts and feelings that he or she believes the speaker is sharing. Unfortunately, filters can prevent the speaker from delivering the message clearly and concisely. Age, gender, cultural differences, educational differences, and belief systems of both the speaker and listener are common filters. Also, speakers often disguise their real intentions for fear of hurting others or using words inappropriately. As a result, the listener may only be able to partially decode the message.

To complicate the process further, just as the speaker may encode inaccurately, so may the listener decode inaccurately as a result of his or her own filtering system.

As with paraphrasing, it is helpful to remember that the goal of decoding and feeding back is to communicate to the speaker your understanding of the subtext of his or her message and your acceptance of his or her reality. By providing the speaker with a restatement or reworking of the emotional message, you indicate whether or not you "got it." If the restatement is accurate, the speaker will be encouraged to go on. If the restatement is not correct, the speaker receives the signal to clarify the message more accurately.

When a person transmits a message about emotions, sometimes what is *not* spoken reveals more than what is. True feelings are often revealed more by a gesture, a facial expression, or the tone or volume of voice than by the words. When decoding, it is important to be receptive to both verbal and nonverbal clues.

The following statements are examples of phrases you can use when feeding back to a speaker the emotions you have decoded during your active listening:

"That really *annoyed* you."
"You're *nervous*."
"You seem *frustrated*."

"It sounds like you're *confused* about . . ."
"You look *surprised*."

Moving from Listening to Action

Active listening is a tool that is used to defuse a person's emotions. Giving the person an opportunity to present his or her case without interruption immediately takes the edge off the situation. If the individual was expecting an argument or even a logical rebuttal, he or she will be pleasantly surprised—and encouraged to be less defensive and more cooperative. By analyzing, then feeding back, the content and emotion that come through to you, you convey to the speaker your interest in and empathy for his or her concern. Before you know it, a potential adversary has been turned into a partner.

The model in Figure 5-6[6] shows how, by carefully gauging his or her own behavior to that of the speaker, a listener can direct the course of the conversation to a positive outcome.

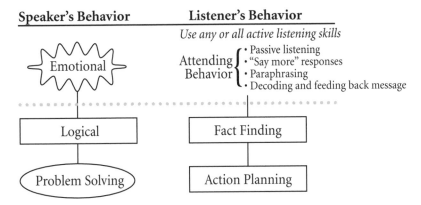

Figure 5-6. When another person's needs are pressing: moving from listening to action planning.

In the upper third of the model, the listener lets the speaker vent. Using active listening skills, he or she draws the speaker out, encouraging open communication but not leading the witness. The listener performs a reality check by paraphrasing the content, decoding, and feeding back the emotional portion of the message.

Once both parties are clear about the message being sent, the listener, through his or her subsequent behavior, can help the speaker to take ownership and responsibility for the issue and, eventually, to find a solution. It is at this point that some of the dirty dozen are redeemed. Although tactics such as threatening, moralizing, name calling, or withdrawing are never acceptable, once the facts have been uncovered, the listener can question, advise, use logical arguments, or praise to get the speaker thinking about solutions. Steering the speaker toward an action plan to resolve the issue is not only appropriate but also desirable at this point in the interaction.

II. Using Assertion Skills

In the second scenario—when *your* needs are pressing— assertion skills are the solution. The trick here is maintaining that delicate balance between standing up for what you value and believe while respecting the needs of others.

The nonassertive individual, in effect, says, "I've got needs and so do you, but I'm not telling you what mine are. And if you don't guess them, I'm going to hold it against you." The nonassertive individual is Mount Saint Helens waiting to erupt. At the other extreme, the aggressive individual proceeds on the basis that " I've got needs and, at best, so do you, but mine count more." This is the schoolyard bully in business attire.

It is crucial to recognize the proper boundaries for each of the three behaviors on the continuum. Boundaries may be either physical or psychological. Physical boundaries refer to variables that are tangible and quantifiable. If another person's behavior costs you money or wastes your time, your physical boundaries have been invaded. Psychological boundaries refer to variables that are intangible and more difficult to quantify. They can include people trying to control you, making decisions for you, second-guessing your decisions, or going over your head to your boss with their issues.

People who are nonassertive, for example, must learn how to protect their boundaries—whether physical or psychological—and express their agenda without crossing the line to aggression. The aggressive individual, in contrast, must learn not to violate the boundaries of other people.

As was stressed earlier, each behavior on the continuum has payoffs, and each exacts a price. For the nonassertive executive, the payoff is avoiding arguments and coming across as a team player. But the price is steep in terms of unmet needs and diluted effectiveness. Aggressive executives tend to get their way and benefit from the charisma of machismo. They pay the price, however, in alienating other people, closing down input and feedback, and failing to gain commitment, especially in the new knowledge-based organization.

Being assertive forces compromise and takes patience and time, but it has all the benefits of a win-win approach.

Skills for the Art of Assertion

The vice president of marketing for a New York cosmetics giant was not having fun. She was hardworking, hard-driving, and deeply committed to getting results. But her department was plagued by turnover and, increasingly, her peers on the senior management team ran the other way rather than face the possibility of being assigned to a project or task force with her. She did not work well cross-functionally, and she became increasingly isolated. As talented as she was, her manager felt that she was becoming a liability. Either she "dialed down" her behavior or she faced being jettisoned.

In another case, the vice president of operations in a Midwest manufacturing organization occupied the other extreme. He was the ultimate nice guy. He was a good delegator but felt uncomfortable holding his employees accountable for results. He found it difficult to be directive and was a poor coach. His people exhibited little sense of urgency, and work fell between the cracks. His typical response was, "I want to respect my people." Clearly, this vice president's behavior had to be "dialed up" to improve his level of play.

Ms. Dial Down and Mr. Dial Up clearly required coaching. Ms. Dial Down needed to become a better listener and improve her ability to understand and deal with resistance without creating enemies. Mr. Dial Up needed to become more assertive and more willing to confront.

Each had to learn the skills that would enable them to move toward the midpoint of assertion, including persistence, sidestepping, straight talk, and the three-part "I" response.

Let's take a closer look at each of these skills and how they can help you move your behavior along the continuum.

1. *Persistence.* How do you make it clear to someone who is trying to invade your boundaries that such behavior is unacceptable? By being persistent. By repeating the same response, over and over, until they get the point. For example, you might keep saying, "I have a concern about what you just said."

This is a tricky technique because it is designed to avoid engagement. It is often difficult to carry out with someone close to you. It works best with people with whom you are not trying to cultivate lasting relationships, such as salespeople, contribution seekers, and telemarketers. No matter whom you attempt to use it on, be polite and gracious, but do not allow them to trap you into giving reasons or explaining why you must say no. Simply sound like a broken record!

2. *Sidestepping.* Use this technique when you want to end a discussion or avoid an argument. When people begin to debate

any subject about which they have strong feelings, emotions quickly take over. Remember, what is said in the heat of the moment cannot be taken back and can seriously impair a relationship. Whether in the workplace or outside of it, there are times when it behooves you to dial down your response. Side-stepping can help you to emerge gracefully from a potentially explosive situation.

When you sidestep, you acknowledge that the other person might have a good point. You simply say, "You may be right" or "That's certainly a possibility," and refuse to argue any further. Saying these words does not mean you are admitting that you are wrong or that you agree with the other person, but it does defuse the situation.

3. *Straight Talk.* Straight talk is a powerful, direct, and open means of communicating your wants and needs. Use it when you want to modify another person's behavior to get your needs met. To ensure the other person understands what you are saying when you use straight talk, be specific and concise. Put your statement into the following format:

I want/need . . . .   because . . . .

For example, "I want you to supply me with the financial data before noon because I must have my report completed by 5 P.M." Or, "I need you to approve the new package design by the end of the week, because it is going into production on Monday."

Combining your request with a reason conveys the idea that you respect the other person enough to feel that he or she deserves an explanation. It prevents you from being perceived as aggressive. It turns what may have been construed as a command into a request, making people more willing to honor it. It is an excellent way to raise the other person's level of cooperativeness.

Unfortunately, many people will not take no for an answer or tune out information that is not welcome. With these individuals, both sidestepping and straight talk might need to be combined with persistence to get the point across.

4. *The Three-Part "I" Response.* This technique is the most powerful—and the most difficult—of the assertiveness techniques. It is used when you are not getting what you want or when you are getting what you do not want. It is designed to protect your boundaries and to change other people's behavior. Unlike simple persistence, which is most useful when you are not terribly concerned about alienating the individual, you want to use this technique with people whom you know well and with whom you have a long-standing, important relationship.

The three-part "I" message comprises three distinct parts:

A description of the troublesome behavior	The disclosure of your feelings + about the behavior	The effect it has on + you

When you deliver the message, it is more effective if you use the following formulation:

When you . . .	+ I feel . . .	+ because . . .

For example, "When you don't give me the financial data on time, I feel nervous and pressured because I still have to complete my report by the deadline." Or, "When you aren't available to approve a design, I feel frustrated because I can't move the project to the next stage."

The "I" part of the message is especially important. A "you" message blames the other party and is likely to trigger defensive behavior. An "I" message isn't likely to be viewed as a personal attack the way a "you" message is. By using the "I" formulation, the speaker accepts full responsibility for his or her reaction to the behavior.

When you give others the opportunity to examine their own behavior in a nonthreatening atmosphere, they tend to be more willing to change their behavior to meet your needs. And that, after all, is your goal when you assert yourself.

A particularly powerful way to assert yourself when someone has violated your boundaries is to combine a three-part "I" response with straight talk. The "I" message lets the other person know that you have an issue with his or her behavior and explains, clearly and in a depersonalized way, what that issue is. The straight talk communicates the change in behavior that you would like to see the person make going forward.

For example: "When you don't give me the financial data on time, I feel nervous and pressured because I still have to complete my report by the deadline. I want you to supply me with the financial data before noon because I have to have my report completed by 5 P.M." Or, "When you aren't available to approve a design, I feel frustrated because I can't move the project to the next stage. I need you to approve the new package design by the end of the week, because it is going into production on Monday."

In addition to rethinking her body language, Sheila Hopkins learned to use the three-part "I" response, in conjunction with straight talk, to successfully influence at least one of her direct reports. She recounts:

> I have a direct report who is a remarkably bright young man and a very proactive thinker. Unfortunately, he is short-tempered and gets visibly angry when things don't go his way. After being trained in assertion skills, I decided to be very direct with him: to tell him which behavior was problematic for me, why it was so, and what I

needed him to do differently. "John," I said, "When you get really angry and begin to yell, it is a big problem for me because it makes me think you are really hard to work with and not a team player. I need you to maintain your cool and your composure all of the time because it is the professional thing to do." This approach was very really effective; John has made an effort to turn his behavior around, and there were no hard feelings after our discussion.

Assertiveness Can't Hurt

Many team members—especially the junior ones—fear that by being assertive they will alienate their superiors. They do not want to come across as pushy, egotistical, or lacking in respect for those with more experience. They worry that their assertiveness will be perceived as aggressiveness. However, becoming assertive is one of the best ways to gain the respect of both peers and senior management.

When you refuse to allow others—no matter what their level or experience—to walk over you, you establish yourself as a force to be reckoned with. By asserting yourself, you demonstrate your commitment to the success of the team. People recognize that you are engaged in the game and willing to play for the high stakes. By refusing to allow other people to ignore your needs, you ensure that you will not be ignored.

III. Using Conflict-Management Skills

❐ The vice president of marketing for North America wants to introduce new packaging for a pharmaceutical product. Making the change worldwide would result in large savings and make it easier to sell his idea to upper management, but his counterpart in Europe isn't buying in.

❏ The head of finance has developed a new format for monthly reports, which he wants all departments to follow. "No way," says the sales director. "I prefer the old format."

❏ Two executives share the services of an administrative assistant, and each wants 75 percent of the person's time. Too bad she doesn't have a twin.

In each of these situations, two people have needs that are in opposition, and each is determined to prevail. This is a powder keg waiting to be ignited, and defusing it will require the full range of conflict-management skills.

Chapter 1 discussed in detail the four options that are available for dealing with conflict:

1. *Play the victim.* Say nothing, act powerless, and complain.

2. *Leave.* Physically remove oneself from involvement

3. *Change oneself.* Move off one's position, shift one's view of the other party, or let it go.

4. *Confront.* Address the issue openly, candidly, and objectively; communicate with the other party.

Option one is never viable. Playing the victim generally exacerbates a situation by sweeping conflict under the carpet. It causes hard feelings and delays the inevitable. The second option is often unavailable. Besides, conflict is inevitable, and you need to learn methods for dealing with it. Changing yourself is fine, but don't count on being able to do it. The question is: What price are you willing to pay?

This leaves confronting as the most effective way to resolve issues without igniting thermonuclear war. We recommend using an overall strategy for confronting, which we call The Four C's Approach.

The Four C's for Confronting

The four C's that make up this strategy are:

1. *Connecting.* Establishing a rapport with the other party by (a) addressing the issue between you openly and candidly and (b) asserting yourself.
2. *Clarifying.* Seeking to understand by (a) active listening and (b) exploring all points of view.
3. *Confirming.* Reaching mutual agreement as to what each party wants and needs and establishing your willingness to collaborate.
4. *Contracting.* Negotiating agreements for future interaction.

While carrying out this conflict-resolution strategy, you will use some of the techniques mentioned previously, such as assessing your style and your colleagues' methods of dealing with conflict, active listening skills, and assertiveness skills.

Let's discuss each element of the confronting strategy in more detail:

1. *Connecting.* Before attempting to connect with another person—to establish a rapport that is conducive to discussing your mutual needs—always check with the person to determine the best time and place to have your discussion. Don't forget attending behavior: Ensure that you have privacy, will not be interrupted, are in a neutral, nonthreatening environment, and have scheduled enough time to cover all salient points, and that both of you have had enough time to prepare for your meeting.

Finding the correct words to begin a potentially adversarial discussion can be difficult. We suggest using partnering phrases, which convey the idea that you are ready to address the issue candidly and objectively, and that you are serious about resolving it. For example:

❏ "I have some concerns about the way we are making decisions that I'd like to explore with you."

❏ "I have an issue with your attendance, and we can't afford to let this go unresolved."

❏ "We seem to have some fundamental differences about how to market the new product, and I'd like to address these with you."

❏ "I am having some difficulties with the way you are managing the IT project. They're really going to get in the way if we don't deal with them."

❏ "I'm uncomfortable with your approach to performance reviews, and I want to work my concerns out with you."

2. *Clarifying.* Clarifying is a critical step in conflict management. Until both parties are clear about one another's issues, it is impossible to negotiate, or contract, a mutually satisfying agreement. This is the ideal place to begin using your active listening skills to encourage the other party to open up about the real issues he or she has. Assertion skills will also help you to describe the behaviors you are concerned about and the reasons you find them troubling.

Once again, choosing the correct words is crucial. Try these clarifying phrases:

❏ "Let's take a minute to clarify what we hear each other saying about the way we've been making decisions."

❏ "It is important for me to understand where you're com-

ing from. What do I need to know to understand what's
been happening with your attendance?"

❏ "Let's define our key concerns regarding marketing the
new product. How about you expressing your concerns
first, since they are important for me to understand?"

❏ "Regarding the IT project, what feedback do you have
for me about anything I've been doing to contribute to
the situation?"

❏ "I want to know what you think. What is your point of
view on performance reviews?"

3. *Confirming.* Confirming entails summing up the facts,
that is, restating the issues to ensure that nothing has been misunderstood or omitted during your discussion. Equally important is a summary of the emotional progress that has been
made, which is the commitment that you've both made to find
a mutually agreeable solution. Although at this point both parties are usually eager to move to action, investing a few additional minutes in confirming will make the next step much
easier.

Here are confirming statements that executives have found
useful:

❏ "Is there anything we missed that needs to be discussed
regarding the marketing strategy?"

❏ "Here's my understanding of our differences and where
we are right now on the issue of the IT project."

❏ "Do you have any other concerns about our performance reviews?"

❏ "I really appreciate your willingness to work through this
issue with me."

❏ "I'm optimistic that we can find a win-win solution
here."

4. *Contracting.* Contracting is the final stage in managing conflict by confronting. It entails finding the win-win solution that both parties have committed to. At this point, one of the most effective tools available to executives is the combination of the three-part "I" response and straight talk that we recommended as a way of asserting yourself.

Let's take the example of two IT executives responsible for the rollout of an enterprise resource planning (ERP) system. In the past two weeks, Deborah, the project manager, has authorized overtime to keep the project on schedule. Sam, her boss, has recently learned about the overtime from another manager. Sam's combination three-part "I" response, combined with straight talk, might sound something like this:

> Deborah, when you authorize overtime without telling me, you put me in a difficult situation. I'm the one who's responsible for staying on budget, and if there are any cost overruns, I'm the one who'll have to explain them. From now on, I need you to come to me before authorizing any overtime on the ERP rollout.

At this point, Deborah is likely to retort with an explanation of her behavior, such as:

> You were away for the weekend; you said you couldn't be reached; and I had to make the call. I figured because you didn't give me your phone number, you didn't want me to bother you. If you want to make the decisions, I have to be able to get in touch with you.

Touché! Now Deborah is the one asserting herself, making it clear that she, too, has needs. The negotiation will now proceed, back and forth, until both Sam's and Deborah's needs are met. If Sam is not willing to give up his privacy by leaving a telephone number, maybe he will agree to call Deborah for a daily update the next time he goes away. Or he may decide to give Deborah more leeway, arranging for her to authorize overtime up to a certain number of hours without his approval.

Some useful contracting phrases are:

- ❐ "I think the whole team needs to be involved in budget decisions. What do you think?"
- ❐ "Having you work four ten-hour days doesn't work for me, but having you come in at 10 A.M. and work until 6 P.M. would. Would that work for you?"
- ❐ "Let's plan some practical next steps to develop the marketing plan together."
- ❐ "One thing we can do to move the IT project ahead is . . ."
- ❐ "What would you prefer that I do differently in the future regarding the way I conduct my performance reviews?"

Learning to Let Go

Remember those going-in stories, or preconceived notions that people bring into their interactions? Going-in stories are a major obstacle to successful conflict management and often prevent people from taking the first step toward resolving their differences. Learning to let go of these destructive stories is one of the keys to conflict resolution.

When individuals are serious about contracting to resolve their differences, they must be willing to take responsibility for their respective going-in stories.

Most two-way conversations are fertile ground for going-in stories. Take this situation: You and I are talking about an issue that is important to me, when you suddenly look at your watch. In reality, all I know is that you looked at your watch. But, as so often happens, I may take that objective event and create a story—a subjective interpretation—about it. I may say, "Howard is bored with our conversation" or "Howard doesn't think my concern is important." Then, based on the story I have created, I begin to have an emotional reaction. I feel angry or hurt or betrayed. Conflict now exists where there was none before.

How can such scenarios be prevented? By refusing to create the story that led to the negative emotion. Asking people point-blank to tell you why they are engaging in certain behavior, instead of creating a story in a vacuum, is the best way to keep from becoming your own worst enemy. Instead of becoming upset when I looked at my watch, you might have said to me, "Howard, I see you are looking at your watch. What's that about?" I would then have had the opportunity to respond, "I have an appointment across town in half an hour, and I was wondering if I'd have enough time to get there" or "I'm expecting an overseas call at 11 A.M., and I was wondering how much time we have before it comes in" or even "I'm hungry, and I was wondering how long it is until lunch." If you had known that my gesture had nothing to do with my feelings about you or your issue, you would have short-circuited the going-in story and prevented hard feelings and the possibility of conflict.

The Importance of Conflict-Management Skills

We are programmed from an early age to avoid conflict. Conflict-resolution skills are not part of any high school, college, or business school curriculum that we are familiar with. Yet, the potential for conflict exists whenever we interact with others. As Pat Parenty, senior vice president and general manager of

Redken, U.S.A., points out, "Expecting people to resolve their differences without giving them conflict-management skills is like giving a computer to someone who's never seen one before and saying, 'Have fun using this.'"

Campbell's John Doumani sums up his commitment to conflict-management skills training in these words:

> Looking at conflict situations as part of the job, as a business case, doesn't come easily, but it is critical that people learn how to do it. They also need to become aware of the impact they have on others and to learn how to process the feedback they get from their colleagues. They don't learn these lessons unless you are willing to put a lot of time and energy into modeling the behavior and building the skill base in the organization. We've put in place quite a few conflict-resolution and influence-management training modules—not just for the leadership team, but throughout the organization—as a way to get people moving in the right direction. At first, it was hard for people to change their behavior, but as people practiced the skills, they became second nature. The way our organization views conflict, and deals with it, has really changed.

While this chapter focused on old-fashioned conflict in the social space of an organization, what kind of skills are required for dealing with conflict in the wired organization of the twenty-first century? That is the subject of Chapter 6.

Notes

1. Adapted from Kenneth Thomas, "Conflict and Conflict Management," *The Handbook of Industrial and Organizational Psychology*, Marvin Dunnette, editor (Chicago: Rand McNally, 1976).

2. Thomas Gordon, *Leader Effectiveness Training: L.E.T.* (New York: Putnam, 1977), p. 272; in the Appendix, the author explains the origin of active listening. The term *active listening* was first suggested to me by Richard Farson. However, the technique itself is derived from the work of Carl Rogers and his psychology students at Ohio State University. At that time, it was labeled "reflection of feelings."

3. Gordon, *Leader Effectiveness Training: L.E.T.* , pp. 60–63.

4. Both the active listening techniques outlined here and the assertion skills discussed later in this chapter are not original with Guttman Development Strategies. Because they have been used by many others, for many years, we are unable to trace them with certainty to their originators.

5. Adapted from the sender/receiver model described in Gordon, *Leader Effectiveness Training: L.E.T.*, pp. 51–52.

6. The concepts illustrated in this model were developed by Bernard M. Kessler, Ph.D.

CHAPTER 6

E-Conflict

"E-mail [is] the killer app of the Wired Age. Executives see it as an invaluable means of communicating with far-flung offices and employees. But the pain of dealing with e-mail has caused many to ask whether the killer app will kill them, too."[1]

Consider these news items:

❏ On the World Wide Web: An "Internet Shootout" is under way, with Israeli and/or Jewish hacker attacks aimed at Palestine's, Hezbollah's, and other Arab Web sites. Arabs counterattack by targeting the Web sites of the Israeli Army, foreign ministry, prime minister, and Knesset.

❏ On eBay: A Lebanese-American woman offers "Palestinian-thrown rocks," with bids starting at $20 for one rock.

❏ In a *Newsweek* article, a young woman describes her first e-mail argument, a disagreement with one of her relatives, in which "our barbs zapped through cyberspace." She states that she didn't know how common e-mail fighting is—until she mentioned it to friends, who "readily confessed their own online tiffs."[2]

So it goes. Old-fashioned, dysfunctional conflict has a way of metastasizing and invading unprotected targets, whatever spaces—social, political, or technological—they may occupy. And, with the unprecedented expansion of electronic communication, the number of conflict targets has grown exponentially.

Two-thirds of the 130 million adult workers in the United States send 3 billion e-mail messages daily, equating to twenty-one messages per electronic mailbox every day. During 2000, the Internet delivered more than 400 billion messages in the United States alone. To put that into perspective, the U.S. Postal Service delivered only 100 billion pieces of mail in the same period![3]

In 2001, the average employee spent between two and two-and-a-half hours per day reading and sending e-mail messages.[4] According to e-mail researcher and consultant David Ferris, the volume of e-mail is expected to grow between 60 and 80 percent in 2002.[5] All of which makes e-communication a huge potential breeding ground for conflict. It is imperative that this ground be secured before the gathering mushroom clouds work their way to the electronic transmissions in your organization.

There is, of course, nothing inherently wrong with e-mail. However, because of the large number of e-mail messages that executives receive—many executives receive from fifty to one hundred messages a day—the speed and ease of response, and the ability to circulate messages with a click, there is great potential for mischief. This potential has been increased by the nearly universal e-mail literacy. Although an organization can become completely wired in a matter of weeks, the ability of its employees to effectively communicate in the new medium may take much longer to develop.

E-mail is not only about speed, efficiency, and information but also about unscreened emotions, opinions not tempered by body language, and thoughts—some hostile and provocative—unrefined by reflection.

E-Mail as a Lethal Weapon

E-mail has eight characteristics that sow the seeds of conflict and discourage people from dealing with it in a healthy, open manner:

1. *E-mail encourages disengagement.* We know that most people shy away from confrontation. E-mail gives them a perfect out. Lois Huggins, vice president of organization development and diversity for Sara Lee Corporation, explains why this is so:

> Conflict makes people feel so uncomfortable generally, and sending e-mails back and forth doesn't feel like engaging. If a conflict-averse person knows there is going to be an issue, using e-mail feels a lot easier than having to sit down and engage in a conflict because e-mail is a one-way tool. You don't have to listen to the response. Also, it's a lot harder to look a person in the eye and say what's on your mind. There are a lot of physiological responses that occur in a face-to-face interaction. You might begin to perspire; you might blush; your facial expression might give away how you feel; your heartbeat might go up; your pulse rate might increase. Many of these reactions can be seen by others,

and a lot of people don't want to be that vulnerable.

E-mail lends itself to dealing in data points and deadlines,
and it provides an easy escape for those unwilling to penetrate
the emotional subtext of an issue. The art of face-to-face communication—and it is an art—takes a back seat to the terse pre-
sentation of bare facts, leaving recipients of e-mail messages
feeling as though they are merely being given marching orders
or are being manipulated, rather than receiving helpful suggestions or critiques. This is especially true when the sender is the
person's immediate supervisor.

In one such case, the vice president for Southeast Asian operations of a midsize manufacturing organization sent an
e-mail message to one of his employees in Thailand. The e-mail
expressed disappointment in the results of an advertising campaign that the Thai manager had launched and suggested that
an analysis be conducted to determine the cause of the failure.
The Thai manager's response was tinged with sarcasm. It suggested, in effect, that before pointing an accusing finger elsewhere, the vice president should conduct a similar analysis in
his own backyard, Singapore, where the campaign had been
even less successful.

The vice president's e-mail reply was a polite and noncommittal: "Thank you for your reply." The company paid a price
for this disengagement. It never did discover why the advertising campaign went awry, nor was an examination ever conducted of the emotional dissonance that lay below the surface
of the Thai manager's response.

We know an executive who rides the wings of e-mail de-
tachment to an extreme. In his attempt to dodge engagement,
he responds to e-mail messages in a "you said/my response"
format. The "you said" refrain merely restates the sender's message, while the "my response" offers a literal reply, usually in

bulleted format. Although this executive gets points for seeking clarity and precision, his colleagues bristle at the robotic-like responses they receive from him.

2. *E-mail enables people to avoid accountability.* If you are responsible for making a decision or implementing a plan, soliciting ideas and suggestions from your colleagues, in person, can be a tedious chore. E-mail makes it so much easier: Type out the request once, call up a preexisting list of recipients, and hit the send button. It does not matter that many of the people on the list are neither knowledgeable about nor involved in the issue at hand. Since it is so easy to include them, why not do it?

Gerard Kells, vice president of human resources for Johnson & Johnson's medical devices and diagnostics group, refers to this indiscriminate solicitation of input as "using e-mail as a chat room" and says that he "immediately shuts down" when someone tries to involve him in this way:

> Somebody sends out an e-mail to me and 27 other people and says, "I'd appreciate your comments on the following." I'm sitting here, drafting my response, when my e-mail pings. Then it pings a second time, and a third, and a fourth. I can't process all those responses. I can't incorporate answers to them into my response. So I just sit back and see what everyone else has to say. And I suspect that the person who's ultimately responsible for the decision is now as confused as I am.

Spreading out accountability in this way often delays important decisions, says Peter Wentworth, vice president of global human resources for Pfizer Consumer Health Care:

> E-mail allows you to redirect accountability for decisions to somebody else. To diffuse account-

ability. It's one thing for a decision maker to send an e-mail to others asking for a direct answer to a question or for additional information on which to make the decision. But all too often these e-mails are sent out asking for opinions and input into the decision-making process. Decisions that should be made consultatively are suddenly being made by consensus—when they are made at all.

3. *E-mail encourages subterfuge.* Curiously, although e-mail usually encourages a rapid response, it can also prolong response time. We have seen more than a few executives agonize over an e-mail response, editing and reediting it, secretly circulating the e-mail or intended response to colleagues—often in breach of confidentiality—for feedback, guidance, and perhaps even a little old-fashioned character assassination. As one executive complained, many of the e-mails that he receives "come with a tail."

Julia Nenke, former human resources director for Foxtel, recalls one instance in which a colleague tried to "put one over on her" electronically:

> A manager sent me an e-mail in which he made a case for a salary increase for one of his staff. Normally, performance is reviewed once a year and raises given at the time of the review. Nowhere in the e-mail did the manager include the information that the employee had been reviewed and received an increase six months prior. This fact would probably have come out if we had discussed the case in person, but because it wasn't mentioned in the message I wasn't aware of it, and I approved the increase.

Such sins of omission are common in wired organizations, as are attempts to sow electronic seeds of dissension. One executive from the health care industry calls messages that are sent to discredit others "heat-seeking missiles," which people use as weapons against one another. He gave us an example of how lethal they can be. At nearly 5 P.M. on a Friday afternoon, one of his managing directors received a call from the field saying that his stock of a critical chemical for conducting assays was depleted. The only way that testing could continue over the weekend was for employees to contact customers who had stock and "borrow" it for those who had run out. The managing director was furious. Instead of picking up the telephone and calling the vice president of operations, who was the responsible party, he went over that individual's head—and over the head of the president of operations as well. He sent an e-mail to the chair and the international president, saying that this was the ninth or tenth time in the last six months that they had run out of stock and asking why no one was "minding the store."

Of course, neither of these two executives had any power to fix the problem. But, feeling duty-bound to respond, they forwarded the managing director's message to several other executives, adding comments such as, "I think the managing director has been incredibly patient," and "Operations has obviously fallen down on the job." The president of operations, who had not been informed of the problem—and whose vice president still knew nothing about it—was one of the recipients of the forwarded messages. When she learned of the managing director's missile strike, she became so upset that she nearly resigned.

E-mail makes it easy to put forward hidden agendas, such as the need to sing one's own praises or make another person look bad, explains one U.S. executive. She has often received "CYA" e-mails: messages that are sent when something has gone wrong, and one person wants to spread the word that he or she is not to blame. "I only made a recommendation; Rebecca made the final decision," or "I tried to tell Marvin he was making a mistake" are typical CYA messages that are sent out, ostensibly, to explain but, in reality, to blame.

4. *E-mail fosters electronic triangulation.* The following example speaks volumes about how easy it is to fall into the electronic triangulation trap. The director of marketing of a financial-services firm worked with an outside consultant on a project to conduct telephone interviews with key customers. The aim was to determine customer-perceived value.

To kick off the project, the division's general manager circulated an e-mail message to his team leaders and to the senior sales reps who reported to them, asking the reps to contact their largest accounts to set up the interviews.

One salesman, with a reputation for backroom shenanigans, e-mailed his team leader telling him to keep the marketing director away from his accounts. He preferred the outside consultant, ostensibly because the consultant was a more seasoned interviewer. In fact, the marketing director was highly regarded throughout the company for his ability to ask insightful questions.

Without much reflection, the team leader forwarded the sales rep's e-mail to the marketing director, who, understandably, became irritated. His relationship with the offending sales rep carried a great deal of baggage, and he was tempted to reply to the sales rep with both barrels, but he decided to lay low. He politely e-mailed the sales rep, with a blind e-copy to the general manager, innocently asking, "Why the concern?" The marketing director knew he would not get an honest response, but that did not matter: His real objective was to draw the general manager into the fray. Classic triangulation!

Sure enough, the sales rep's e-mail response was warily

noncommittal, whereupon the marketing director forwarded it to the general manager with a note saying that this was simply another case of the sales rep's evasiveness and asking the general manager to reprimand the troublemaker. The general manager was eager to accommodate the marketing director because of his own history of unresolved conflict with the sales rep, and he fired off an electronic slap on the wrist.

But triangulation spawns many moves. The sales rep was undeterred by the general manager's e-mail. Rather than cease and desist, he sent a for-your-eyes-only e-mail to the outside consultant, whom he had worked with at a previous employer. The sales rep electronically stroked the consultant for his superior capabilities and implored him to conduct the interviews with his clients.

So, what do you think happened? You guessed it! The outside consultant clicked the forward button and sent the sales rep's message to the marketing director. Compound triangulation!

So it went. The sales rep's clients were never interviewed; the company missed a chance to gather valuable input from several key clients; and the sales rep and marketing director continued to glower at one another in virtual and real space.

5. *Electronic communication popularizes a new sport: tag-team e-mail.* With the availability of e-mail, enlisting supporters for one's own point of view has become easier than ever. Consider this: The executive team of an international consulting firm met to discuss the company's positioning platform. After an initial discussion on the subject, the outside consultant to the team was asked to e-mail an initial draft of the statement to team members, who, in turn, were to make revisions and forward them electronically to the consultant.

One team member, the managing director of the company's European business, suddenly had a flash of inspiration: Why not ask his marketing director to comment on the positioning statement to ensure local "fit"? Her revisions, it turned out, were significant, and the managing director sent her comments, along with his own, to the outside consultant, with electronic copies forwarded to his fellow team members.

Not to be outdone, the managing director of Australia-Asia proceeded to follow suit and involve his marketing director. Next, the head of the Latin American operation jumped on the involvement bandwagon and tagged his marketing manager for comment.

Things grew worse. The directors of several staff departments were also asked for comments by the company's executive vice president. Soon, e-mails were whizzing back and forth in almost every permutation: top-team members to one another, staff to staff, staff to top team—you name it, and it was being sent. Each handoff led to more comments, edits, and revisions.

Tempers frayed. The marketing director in Europe was accused by her peers of grandstanding. A top-team member, disgusted by the free-for-all, decided to go off-line and partner with several of his peers to come up with a new draft of the statement. This incensed the outside consultant and angered those senior executives who were excluded. Weeks later, the organization finally came to its senses when the CEO halted the tag-teaming by calling for a face-to-face meeting of his senior executives to review the broken process and set new ground rules.

Susan Fullman, corporate vice president and director of customer solutions and support for Motorola, describes tag-teaming as "exponential dysfunction":

> Where you could have included one or two people, now you are including four people on the e-mail, and now you get four times the dysfunc-

tion. On several occasions I've seen dozens of people copied, and most of them didn't know anything about the subject that was being discussed. In such cases, I try to stop the dysfunction in its tracks by setting up a conference call with the primary players and dealing with the issue then and there.

Fullman is not the only executive who has seen this exponential dysfunction firsthand. Julia Nenke of Foxtel describes a situation in which a vice president of finance sent an e-mail message to his counterparts in marketing, sales, and programming requesting information on which to base pricing decisions for the upcoming year. His original message articulated several assumptions related to pricing, each of which was open to interpretation. When the three vice presidents received the message, they immediately forwarded it to their team members, asking them to comment. Because the information was presented in written form from people in authority, the reaction of these people was that it should be taken as gospel, and suddenly thirty-odd people were commenting on these assumptions as though they were fact.

6. *E-mail engenders bravado.* There may be some deep psychological connection between e-mail and road rage. We certainly do not plan to develop this conceit further, except to say that both automobiles and computers appear to encourage risk taking and aggression.

In the case of e-mail, the remoteness of the communication process may explain why "scud e-mails," as one executive termed them, are launched with great frequency. Nonassertive people often refrain from expressing their point of view because they are afraid of other people's reactions. Without anyone else present to challenge or to criticize their ideas, they find it much easier to make a statement and sometimes go too far in the other direction. Freed of their usual inhibitions, they may voice their opinions too forcefully or include caustic remarks about other people in their e-mail messages. And since already-aggressive people become even more aggressive when surrounded by several thousand pounds of sheet metal, an individual who pulls no punches in person may see no reason to temper his or her remote remarks.

One executive relates how, in his company, electronic communication escalated the disagreement between two colleagues into open warfare. Two divisional presidents with polar-opposite styles simply could not get along, especially at annual planning time, when competition for resources typically devolved into a pitched battle. This was a case of Ms. Analytic versus Mr. Turbo-Emotions. Ms. Analytic was a careful, methodical decision maker. Her counterpart preferred a gut-feeling, shoot-from-the-hip approach. E-mail proved to be the perfect medium for these two adversaries to spar with one another without resolving their underlying differences. Each was aware of the other's Achilles' heel, and each know how to take dead aim at it. The ability to engage in open warfare without ever needing to come face-to-face emboldened both. And the cc's that the combatants attached to each of their electronic missiles ensured that they had an audience. Planning and budgeting became a blood sport.

7. *E-mails cannot be taken back.* Who among us has not hammered out a stiff response to a pointed e-mail message from a colleague and pushed the send button, only to develop an immediate case of remorse? Michael Eisner, chair and CEO of Walt Disney Company, reflected on the gaping pitfalls of e-communication in a speech to students at the University of Southern California:

> I have noticed lately that the intensity of emotions inside our competitive company is higher

than usual. I am convinced this is because of e-mail. I learned early in the hard paper world of the 1970s that when I was annoyed with someone, I should write a memo, then put the memo in my desk drawer and leave it there until the next day. About 99 percent of the time, in the morning, either my anger had passed or I realized that my writing was of insufficient precision to save me from being fired. I then picked up the phone to talk things out with the other person, or I saw the person face-to-face. With e-mail, our impulse is not to file and save, but to click and send.[6]

Clicking and sending, without pausing to consider the consequences, can cause serious damage. One executive recalled the time when she was e-mailing highly sensitive information to a colleague in another department. The information included past performance ratings of several incumbents, suggestions for appropriate next positions for them, and other highly confidential personnel data. When she went to the address box, instead of clicking on her colleague's name, she inadvertently clicked on the address above it, which was the entire division's mailbox. "My blood pressure," she says, "went sky high. I called the IT department, and fortunately it was an antiquated mailbox, so no unintended readers got hold of the information. There were no dire consequences from my mistake, but ever since I have been very, very careful whenever sending out anything confidential."

8. *E-mail neutralizes key conflict-management tools and technologies.* In any conversation, the way things are said is equally important as the words that are spoken, and what is not said is often more important than either. Face-to-face commu-

nication allows the speaker and listener to connect on both the intellectual and physical planes. Real-time active listening provides executives with the opportunity to decode and feed back *both the content and emotion* of the messages they receive.

E-mail, by its very nature, makes the utilization of these tools nearly impossible. How can an executive possibly perceive the subtext of a conversation without seeing the facial expressions and gestures of his or her counterpart? In the black-and-white glare of computer-generated characters, the lyrics may come across loud and clear, but the melody of how the message is spoken and felt is completely lost.

Studies have determined that e-mail has caused executives' listening skills to languish, by creating a physical and psychological chasm between them and their colleagues. These studies also suggest that while users of e-mail have more relationships and contact with people inside and outside their organizations, these contacts are not as strong, nor are they as committed.[7]

Toward E-Conflict Rules of Engagement

As Michael Eisner claims, "E-mail's very virtues also make it dangerous—it is instant, global, quick, and easy. It becomes easy to be rude, easy to use language incorrectly, easy to make stupid mistakes, easy to do irreparable harm."[8]

Electronic communication makes it easy to say your piece and "get out of Dodge" before the bullets start flying. These are the same reasons why e-communication is such a threat to successfully managing conflict.

Without clear protocols, negotiating conflict via computer screen is a handicapped expedition—like trying to find your way around an unfamiliar town with no street signs. It is a journey that can easily lead to frustration and even anger. Yet, e-communication will be with us for a long time. By embracing the following ten steps, many executives have found that both their e-communication skills and their ability to use e-communication as a conflict-management tool have greatly improved:

1. *Use the right medium for the message.* E-mail is an effective tool for *one-way* communication, but it does not lend itself to situations that require *interactive* communication. Lois Huggins, among others, has learned to use e-mail primarily as a way to disseminate information to numerous people. "When you just want to share information, and don't need a response," she says, "e-mail is the quickest, most efficient way to do it."

At Foxtel, says Julia Nenke, several protocols have been developed to prevent e-mail from being used inappropriately. Foxtel regards e-mail as a communication, not a decision-making vehicle. Team decisions are made interactively—in person, on the telephone, or during videoconferences. Information relating to decisions that have yet to be made is not to be disseminated electronically. Executives are discouraged from soliciting input, engaging in discussions about alternatives, or putting forth their points of view in e-mails.

It is also unacceptable at Foxtel to use e-mail to either raise an issue of concern/conflict or to engage in negotiations. The reason is that face-to-face communication is three-dimensional. It embraces content, emotion, and both spoken and body language. The subtleties and nuances of conversation not only go a long way toward clarifying a point but can also make or break a negotiation that is conflict-related. Often, the expression on a person's face at the negotiating table will provide telltale clues to his or her willingness to compromise. It is tough to gain (or convey!) the same assurance from an electronically delivered statement of objectives, or similar negotiation platform. As one CFO explains: "Nine times out of ten a conflict is

more easily resolved by face time than by playing dueling
e-mails for weeks on end."

E-mail *is* vitally important in today's high-speed business
climate, but more important is knowing when and when not to
use it. When managing or attempting to resolve conflict, picking up the telephone can be more beneficial than merely clicking the send button.

2. *Substitute active-reading skills for active-listening skills.*

❒ *Get a fix on the sender.* Remember the matrix for framing
strategies discussed in Chapter 5? If you receive a particularly
sensitive e-mail, do not forget to position the sender on that
matrix before attempting to respond. Ask yourself: "What has
my experience with Marcia told me about how she relates to
me? Is she a double-dealer, a foe, a member of the loyal opposition, or a partner?" Then, see what cues you can pick up from
the e-mail that either reinforce your original estimation of Marcia or indicate that her position on the matrix has changed. If
Marcia has always been a foe of yours, and her most recent
e-mail indicates that she continues to take an adversarial stance,
no electronic response is likely to resolve your differences. Your
strategy needs to include voice-to-voice or, better yet, face-to-
face communication.

❒ *Keep the "dirty dozen" out of your responses.* Remember
the dirty dozen responses described in Chapter 5 of sending solutions, evaluating, and withdrawing? All these responses interfere with open, honest communication between speaker and
listener, both in person and electronically. The same rules we
outlined for their use in face-to-face communication apply to
e-mail. Resist the temptation to reply to a person's message
with advice, judgmental remarks, or disinterest. Instead, decode
and feed back the message as you interpret it or ask for further
clarification, using the following active-listening techniques:

(a) *Test your understanding of e-mail messages on two levels.* One of the first principles of active listening is the importance of decoding not only the content of a message but also the emotion behind it. The recipient of an e-mail message needs to do the same. First, ask yourself: "Is the *content* of this message clear?"

This can be a challenge. The vital subtext of an idea or directive, which can often only be perceived by tools such as active listening or strategic framing, can be lost entirely when the message is reduced to a matter of bytes and pixels. You may need to read between the lines. For example, if the e-mail message relates to a problem, ask yourself: "Is the sender trying to determine the cause? Does the sender want me to supply information to help in the search for the cause? Am I being asked to take or recommend corrective action to remove the cause of the problem?"

Next, step back and take a wide-angle view of the message. Ask yourself, "What are the *underlying feelings* being conveyed or implied? Do I detect frustration, anger, or confusion? If so, are these feelings being directed at me or at my area of responsibility?" Now you are better positioned to respond.

(b) *Feed the messages back to the sender for confirmation.* When we read an e-mail message that has been sent to us, we do not have the opportunity to engage in the subtle testing and probing that is possible in real-time discussions. So, before crafting a response, we may need to feed back to the sender both elements of the message—what has been said and what you think was meant—so he or she can confirm that we have understood it properly. We are not recommending the rigid "you said/my response" format of the robotic executive mentioned earlier. Rather, something like, "The message I received from your e-mail is that you want to be involved in the selection of the new IT vendor. The sense I get is that you are upset because you weren't asked to be on the team that will make the decision. Is this correct?"

If the e-mail message you received is muddled, it might be better not to try to divine the message. Instead, send back an e-mail asking for clarification. Ask questions such as, "What do you mean by _____? Can you be more specific? Can you give me any examples of _____? What else concerns you about _____?"

❐ *Deliver* your *messages clearly.* When you are the sender of an e-mail message, identify the goal of your message. Ask yourself, "What's the purpose of this e-mail? Will it prompt the receiver to think or act differently? Am I communicating to inform or to persuade?"

Once you are clear about the goal of your message, you can use the subject line like a banner headline in a newspaper, warming up the recipient with a clear and concise message stating the purpose of your communiqué. Proper labeling also makes it easier for the recipient to glance at his or her inbox and identify your message as worthwhile reading. For example, if your e-mail is a request for action, state that action up front: "ACTION: SEND YOUR EDITS OF THE ATTACHED COPY TO ME BY FEBRUARY 1ST."

It is important to remember that using an e-mail to express a concern and ask a person to change his or behavior is dicey business. If a face-to-face meeting cannot be arranged, a telephone call is preferable to an electronic message. But *if there is absolutely no way in which you can initiate a dialogue*—for example, you are about to board an airplane for the other end of the world; you work days and the other party works nights—and you feel that you have no choice but to transmit your message via e-mail, keep in mind the value of straight talk and three-part "I" responses.

Depersonalize your concern; do not blame the other party for it; explain why you have a problem with his or her behavior; suggest an alternate behavior that you can both agree on.

Let's say that you are out of town, and one of your direct reports has sent you an e-mail informing you that he has missed the deadline to submit your department's travel budget to the finance department. An appropriate electronic reply might be: "When you miss deadlines like this, I am embarrassed because it gives others the impression that our department is badly managed. I'm also concerned that because we are late our budget might not be approved, and we won't have the money we need to do our job. I need you to work overtime tonight and get the figures to finance first thing in the morning."

❐ *There's no need to tell the world.* Finally, choose recipients carefully. With the objective of your message clearly in mind, consider the most appropriate recipients. Ask yourself: "Which people need the information I am sending? Do I need them to think or do something differently as a result of my e-mail?" If not, maybe there's no reason for them to receive your message.

3. *Practice the Golden Rule.* Put yourself mentally in front of the recipient's computer screen. Ask yourself, "How would I

react to the message coming across the screen? Would the message be clear? Would I know what action, if any, I was being asked to take? What feeling or emotion would the message be likely to engender in me?" In other words, think before you send.

Part of practicing the Golden Rule is being sensitive to other cultures. When dealing internationally, for example, take care to eliminate Americanisms and colloquialisms from your writing. Phrases such as "You really hit a home run with that last report" are probably out of place in communications with countries where baseball is not the national sport. And, if it is already afternoon in the country to which you are writing, do not start your message with "Good morning."

After receiving negative feedback about e-mails sent by his direct reports to one of his company's international divisions, one U.S. executive instituted a new protocol that he must review any e-mail before it is sent internationally. It might seem as though this would slow things down, but it has already saved his group from at least one embarrassing situation:

> We were planning an executive-development workshop at which we had reserved a certain number of places for employees in our six North American divisions and our one international group. We had already received the names of the people who would be coming from our domestic operations, but we hadn't yet been told the names of the individuals who would be filling the three slots we had reserved for international employees. One of my direct reports drafted an e-mail to the international manager saying, "We have only three slots left in our workshop. Whom do you want to attend?" When I read it, I realized that it sounded as though we had al-

ready asked everyone else, and because we hadn't filled three slots we had decided to offer the "leftovers" to the international employees. When the writer realized how the draft could have been interpreted, he rewrote it, explaining that we were inviting three people from each division—including international.

Most people do not have someone to provide coaching on their e-mails, but everyone can follow an approach used by Lois Huggins and screen themselves by reading their e-mails aloud. Huggins believes that you market yourself with every e-mail you send, so you should be certain that you are projecting the image you want others to have of you. As she reads aloud, she asks herself, "What's the tone of the message I'm sending? Could that word be misinterpreted? Are the sentences too long? Are there blocks and blocks of text with no space? Will it be difficult for people to read? Will they lose interest?"

4. *Respect confidentiality.* A breach here is a trust-buster. Never, ever pass along a confidential e-mail to anyone not authorized to read it. It is also important to understand that there is no privacy on the Internet: Anything and everything can be discovered with the right tools in the wrong hands. A security breach could result in hackers having access to sensitive materials, and confidential plans can reach the competition through e-mail. *All* sensitive and confidential information should be delivered face-to-face. One IT company in New England went as far as purchasing a fleet of helicopters to fly its employees around the region for face-to-face conferences when key business plans were to be discussed.[9] A little extreme? Maybe so, but the planning process in this organization proceeded without the usual rancor and delay.

5. *Know when—and when not—to "cc."* Top-management teams should agree on ground rules for keeping others in the

cc loop. Protocols need to be developed to address the cc issue not only for e-mail sent within the top-management team but also for messages sent to other managers across functions. When in doubt, reach agreement with those involved before you cc and hit the send button. Likewise, only use cc for your e-mail when it is absolutely necessary for these people to be kept informed.

Use the reply-to-all feature sparingly. Technology makes it much easier, but not necessarily more effective, to communicate with many more people at the same time. Ask yourself, "Do all these people really need to hear my answer? Why don't I respond only to the sender of the message?"[10]

6. *Don't retain a rescuer.* Do not circulate to a third party an e-mail that you have received, and then have that individual join in the response. Deal one-on-one. Otherwise, you will fall into the deadly triangulation trap. The one exception is when you receive permission from the e-mail sender to broaden involvement.

A common, yet subversive, way in which people enlist rescuers is through the "bcc" feature. At Foxtel, says Julia Nenke, sending blind copies was once prevalent, with an estimated 20 percent of e-mail users attaching them to their messages on a routine basis. Within one division, when the senior management team became aware of the practice, they announced that the bcc feature was being removed from the e-mail program. Why? According to Nenke, "Because it was being used to shore up support without the knowledge of the parties who were involved. It was absolutely in conflict with what we were trying to achieve organizationally, which was personal ownership of issues and trust."

7. *Stroke the recipient.* Telemarketing coaches advise their clients to "make sure your voice has a smile." Similarly, executives would be better served if, whenever possible, their e-mail

stroked the recipient. Look for an opportunity to congratulate or thank someone. Remember the executive from Singapore who chastised the manager of his Thailand operation? What if he had begun his e-mail by congratulating the manager on some aspect of the advertising campaign? Perhaps the manager had come in on budget, or the graphics he had used were exceptional. If the vice president had taken this approach, it is likely that he would have received a different reply to his e-mail.

Lois Huggins suggests using e-mail to "bury the hatchet." She has seen situations in which there has been a strained relationship between two people, and, when the conflict has eased, one of the parties has sent an e-mail to the other thanking or congratulating the former adversary: "Thanks so much for the work you did on the marketing plan; you and your team were tremendously helpful to us," or "Congratulations! I heard you got the XYZ account." And, unlike instances in which people copy others to triangulate or put another person down, in these cases it is totally appropriate to send a copy to other members of the department or unit. This communicates to all the other people who may have known in the past that there was a conflict between you that the relationship has improved. It also sends the subtle hint that maybe some of the other warring parties in the organization should follow your example.

8. *Get to know your e-mail correspondents.* Michael Morris of the Stanford Business School and several other academics have studied mock negotiations that use only e-mail and compared them with those that were preceded by a brief getting-to-know-you telephone call. Not surprisingly, the second type went far more smoothly.[11]

Electronic communications are often easier when the correspondents begin by swapping photographs and personal details or when they already know each other. If you routinely correspond with outside vendors, people on other shifts, or employees of other departments or divisions, why not take some time to introduce yourself in person? If you are making a trip to see the corporate HR staff, why not stop in and say hello to the purchasing agent you have only "spoken" to through your computer? Or, if you need to work overtime one night, why not walk into the plant and say hello to the night production supervisor?

Being able to match a face with a name makes it easier to infuse your electronic correspondence with a friendly, more personal tone.

9. *When in Doubt, Don't.* Take Michael Eisner's advice of suspending your response, especially when you are angry or upset. Instead, write the message, hit the save button, and then send it to your own e-mail address. Wait twenty-four hours, then open and reread the message. How would it come across if you were the recipient? If it passes the content-and-feelings litmus test, go ahead and send it.

10. *Pack a parachute.* Do not be afraid to bail out of e-mail, especially when you sense the undertow of strong emotion. Before the situation deteriorates—before misunderstandings escalate and harsh messages are exchanged—that is the time to suggest getting together by telephone or in person.

Check Before You Send

The vast majority of electronic messages that executives receive are relatively routine. But there are some that qualify as "smoking e-mails," which have the potential to ignite a full-fledged blaze. These are the ones that require careful handling. We suggest that, while crafting your response to a potentially incendiary e-mail message, you run through the checklist provided in Figure 6-1.

> *If you are the recipient of a "smoking e-mail," the following checklist can help you to defuse it. As you prepare your response, ask yourself these questions:*
>
> √ How do I assess our relationship: Is the sender of this e-mail a double-dealer, opponent, loyal opponent, or partner? Given his/her position, what is the best way to frame your response?
>
> √ What information is the sender trying to convey? What feelings are behind the message?
>
> √ Do I need to ask the sender for clarification before I can respond?
>
> √ How can I best paraphrase the sender's message so that he/she is aware that I've gotten both the objective and emotional messages?
>
> √ Is my response clear and to the point? If I want the recipient to take action, is that clearly stated up front?
>
> √ Have I stated my case/made my requests in an objective, nonjudgmental way, or does my response contain hidden messages and veiled accusations?
>
> √ Are the language and references that I have used appropriate, given the ethnic background, religion, and physical location of the person I'm responding to?
>
> √ Does my response include any confidential information that should not be shared with the individual to whom I'm writing?
>
> √ How would I react if I were the recipient of this response?
>
> √ Who, *if anyone*, should receive a copy of my response? Why do I want him/her/them to see my response? What will be the possible repercussions if I send copies to these people?
>
> √ Is there any way in which I can make my response friendlier or more personal?
>
> √ Would it be appropriate to include some positive feedback in my response?
>
> √ Is the response I'm preparing more likely to increase or decrease the tension level between me and the sender?
>
> √ Would it be better to try to resolve this issue over the telephone or in a face-to-face meeting than in an e-mail?

Figure 6-1. Checklist for preparing e-mail responses.

End Note

Like conflict, e-mail is here to stay. It has the ability to quickly and cost-effectively facilitate communication within an organization, and it offers the power to help move an idea from conception to reality. How this power is harnessed by senior executives ultimately determines whether electronic communication functions as an indispensable tool for effectively managing disagreement or as a divisive breeding ground for conflict, full of opportunities for subversive and culture-cracking behavior.

When used appropriately, e-communication can serve the purpose of facilitating conflict resolution. Consider, for example, how one culinary union used online mediation during its recent contract negotiations with two major convention centers in Chicago. According to labor counsel Stuart R. Korshak, a partner in the San Francisco–based law firm of Korshak, Kracoff, Kong and Sugano, the two sides reached out to each other via a network of computers and customized software that federal mediators used to help solve labor disputes. Through a specially designed Web site, both the convention center owners and the union were able to view master proposals, the tentative agreements, each side's notes, lists of open issues, and other agreements for the purposes of comparison and to participate in a chat line. Although the negotiations certainly were not easy, they proceeded without the usual e-mail scud-missile attacks and collateral damage that frequently accompany contract negotiations. In fact, agreement was reached partly because of electronic communication.[12]

An important step for senior executives to take toward making e-mail an ally of the top team's effort to manage conflict effectively is moving to change the e-mail paradigm. The same rules and protocols that apply to real-life conflict resolution need to be incorporated into the organization's e-mail etiquette—that is, no subterfuge, no veiled barbs or weasel wording, and no triangulation. In other words, openness, candor, and depersonalization should be exercised during electronic encounters, exactly as they are in team meetings.

As with managing conflict in real time, it is equally important in virtual time to break through those barriers that interfere with effective communication. Recipients should engage in active reading and responding. Specificity is vital: "Here's what I'm getting from your e-mail. Here's what I see as the next steps. Do you agree?"

Despite its challenges and pitfalls, e-mail can become an important resource for top-team members to send and receive clear messages from one another, confront issues fairly and openly, and keep everyone focused on winning where it counts—that is, against competitors in the marketplace.

Notes

1. Alex Salkever, "E-Mail: Killer App—or Just a Killer?" *Business Week* online, March 1, 2002.

2. Candy Schulman, "E-Mail: The Future of the Family Feud?" *Newsweek,* December 18, 2000, p. 14.

3. Gerald Goldhaber, "E-Mail: Tool or Torment?" *Communication World,* vol. 18., no. 5, August 1, 2001, p. 25.

4. Ibid.

5. Salkever, op. cit.

6. Michael Eisner, "E-Communication," *Executive Excellence,* vol. 17, no. 11, November 2000, p. 6.

7. Goldhaber, op cit.

8. Eisner, op cit.

9. Goldhaber, op cit.

10. Goldhaber, ibid., p. 28.

11. "Negotiating by E-Mail," *The Economist,* April 8, 2000, p. 63.

12. Brenda Palk Sunoo, "Hot Disputes Cool Down in Mediation," *Workforce,* vol. 80, no. 1, January 2001, p. 49.

CHAPTER 7

Leadership in Conflict Management

Liz O'Brien has a dirty little secret. She likes the 6 P.M. to 8 P.M. part of her workday best.

That's when everyone else has gone home, her phone doesn't ring, and she can concentrate on sending out e-mails and voice-mail directives to those who work for her at the San Diego Mediation Center.

And, she sheepishly admits this is wrong.

The president of the mediation center is falling into the same trap that many other [leaders] have. She is trying to avoid conflict and perform her job as efficiently as possible.[1]

Much has been written about leadership, including the traits a person must possess and the behaviors he or she must exhibit to inspire confidence and loyalty in other people. In *Reframing Organizations*, Lee Bolman and Terry Deal say that, when people are asked what leadership is, answers seem to fall into one of four categories:

1. The use of power to get others to do what you want
2. The ability to motivate people to get things done
3. The ability to provide a vision to others
4. The empowerment of others to get them to do what you want[2]

The focus, in each case, is on action—that is, on pursuing goals and getting others to pursue them along with the leader.

Other characteristics that are often cited as essential to leaders are the ability to inspire trust and build relationships, the willingness to take risks, self-confidence, interpersonal skills, task competence, intelligence, decisiveness, understanding of followers, and courage.[3]

In these and other summaries of leadership qualities, one essential trait is notably absent, which is the ability to manage conflict. Yet, according to a survey conducted last year by the American Management Association, managers spend at least 24 percent of their workday resolving conflicts. Why then is there a failure to recognize the importance of conflict-management skills?

We can think of two possible explanations. One might be called the rationalistic fallacy. Most literature on leadership focuses on concepts such as visioning, strategy, value creation, organization change, or decision making. You know, arm leaders with a suite of processes to bring these concepts to life, add an analytical component—one of those ubiquitous managerial grids—and success will follow. But reality is far more elusive and not easily susceptible to another person's design or will, no matter how well endowed with "the right stuff" that person may be. Underlying a good deal of organizational life is the undertow of dysfunctional conflict. Ignore this fact, or deal with it ineffectively, and all the step-by-step process solutions and matrix-style analyses will fail to deliver on their promises.

It may also be the case that most pundits—and leaders—

have a fatalistic attitude toward unresolved conflict. It is inevitable. It has always been and will continue to be. Not even the best leader can wipe it out, so why bother? Better to focus on what can be addressed and changed, such as formulating strategy; attending to the elements of the performance system, from goal-setting to seeing to it that key employees are motivated and well trained; becoming the ultimate cheerleader and communicator; being a great role model and coach; and seeing to the care and feeding of key stakeholders. For many people, the idea of involving the leader in the business of redirecting conflict so that it becomes a dynamic force that helps to drive high performance would be tantamount to tilting at windmills!

But neglecting this aspect of leadership is more dangerous than ever before, because of today's global, wired-for-speed business organization, where unresolved conflict has the potential to escalate and permeate the business at the speed of thought. As pointed out earlier, influence, not power, is the new animating organizational force. Leaders can no longer bury conflict by willing it away. They must be at the forefront of conflict, managing it everywhere in the organization.

Lee Chaden, senior vice president of human resources for the Sara Lee Corporation, sums up the power of the leader to set the tone for the entire organization, especially as it relates to conflict management:

> The leader is responsible for the company's tone and the environment in which people work. If the leader is confrontational, divisive, and plays individuals against one another out of the belief that internal competitiveness is a good thing, that *modus operandi* is going to permeate the organization. There is going to be a lot of unconstructive conflict. If, on the other hand, the leader sets a tone of collaboration and teamwork

and makes it clear that that's his value system, that will become the value system of the whole organization.

The Downward Spiral of Maladaptive Leadership: A Case Study

An organization's ability to manage conflict starts with the leader. When that leader is adept at resolving conflict, the rest of the organization will likely follow—as will business results and success. But when the Goliath falls short of the conflict-management mark, so will the Davids below, creating an organization that is self-absorbed and lacking in competitive punch.

One division of a large automobile manufacturer was run by a chairperson who not only couldn't manage conflict but also generated it. For obvious reasons, the company or the executives involved cannot be named. The chairperson—let's call him "Scott"—directed several members of his leadership team to develop a strategy for one of the major segments of the business. The team members remained in continual communication with Scott, seeking his advice and input as they formulated the strategy. All the signals they received from him indicated that they were on the right track.

But reality was different. When the team presented its proposal to Scott and the rest of the management committee, Scott dismissed it summarily. He then proceeded to publicly attack the team members, criticizing their process and the conclusions they had reached. Not surprisingly, the team members were taken aback—until they learned that Scott had clandestinely hired a consulting firm, as a type of shadow quality control check, to carry out the same assignment they had recently completed. The firm's conclusions, it turned out, were significantly different from those of the internal group.

Scott's behavior was clearly maladaptive, and his lack of honesty was only part of the problem. His penchant for restructuring was also problematic. He changed the division's structure, along with reporting relationships, at least once a year. At one point, he divided R&D into two separate functions, only to reunite them soon afterward and have the reconstituted entity report to him. Twelve months later, Scott again stirred the waters. He decided that R&D should report to the division president instead of to him. The constant churn and change had left his management team worn out and demoralized.

Instability is a breeding ground for triangulation. Before long, members of the top team chose the vice president of human resources, "Sandra," to be the go-between, as they attempted to manage Scott and control damage through the ranks. In a typical encounter, one of these senior managers would come to Sandra with a dilemma such as, "Scott told me to do a study on the sale of our minivans in Europe but not to tell Lillian anything about it. She's the one who has all the sales figures, so how do I do it without talking to her?"

In another case, it was 2 P.M. on a Friday when a fellow team member came barreling into Sandra's office, shouting, "You won't believe this. You know the manufacturing problem we've had a team of twenty people sorting out for the past three days? Scott just pulled me out of a meeting and told me to go into the room where they are meeting and tell them that if the problem isn't solved by 5 P.M. today, they're all going to be fired."

Sandra catalogued the maladaptive behaviors that the group began to exhibit in response to Scott's machinations, and the effect these behaviors had on the rest of the organization:

> People started moving into armed camps around certain issues. In meetings, they said nothing: They had become completely risk-averse because no matter what they said, they felt that they were going to be second-guessed. They gave their tacit agreement, then walked out with essentially no commitment to accomplish or do anything. After each meeting, people would break up into small groups, with everybody rolling their eyes and saying, "Can you believe where we ended up?" These corridor conversations really started grating on the rest of the organization. Because the rest of the organization, even if they are not physically present, can tell that their senior management is not aligned.

The consequences of maladaptive behavior at the top can be—and usually are—dire. This case was no exception. Understandably, the top team became inner directed, unable to move beyond the internal strife. The company's sizable R&D investment was being frittered away by false starts, lack of direction, and ineffective discipline, and the constant "rearranging of the deck chairs" that characterized Scott's leadership. The company's sluggish R&D pipeline began to put it at a competitive disadvantage. It was another example of the power of maladaptive leadership to spiral downward.

Although we would like to be able to say that leaders like Scott are the rare exception, the bad news is that, unfortunately, this is not true. Maladaptive leadership is common for several reasons—some having to do with personality and others with power issues—and many leaders simply cannot adapt to a team environment. They have trouble letting go of authority, trusting others, and communicating.

On the other hand, reformation is possible. We have encountered few leaders who have not been able to change. The approaches and techniques outlined in this book have proven to be effective catalysts for personal transformation. This transformation begins, as it does in team-alignment sessions, with a look in the mirror.

The Path to Reformation

Disturbed by the atmosphere within the division and the way in which she was being enlisted by the other members of Scott's team, Sandra contacted the corporate vice president of human resources. She recommended an intervention: basically, an alignment of the senior team and personal coaching for Scott. The corporate vice president suggested she speak with each team member individually, then present a list of their concerns to Scott.

When Sandra sat down with Scott for the first time, he was not happy. After all, Sandra had gone over his head, and the corporate vice president now knew that there were chinks in his armor. Denial is a common reaction of leaders to negative feedback, and Scott was no exception. His initial reaction to the picture of his team's concerns that Sandra began to paint was, "That just isn't me."

Sandra's strategy was wise: Depersonalize the feedback. She proceeded to explain to Scott that, "There is hardly any senior leadership team that doesn't have to work on issues, and this is a common part of a team's development. We have to work on these issues just as we would work on any other business issue." She then proceeded to elaborate, in a dispassionate way, on the areas of confusion that existed within the team, such as a lack of clarity around roles and responsibilities, people not knowing where to go for approvals, where the decision-making power resided, and where strategy was being formulated.

As Sandra spoke, it became apparent that Scott hadn't realized how much confusion and strife his behavior had caused. And Sandra pointed out that the responsibility for the situation was not all his. Team members had failed to confront Scott directly. They had chosen, instead, to go underground with their dissatisfaction. Scott, to his credit, listened to Sandra's reasoning and accepted her recommendation that the team devote time and energy to realigning itself. This required Scott to sit through another feedback session, this time with the entire team present and answering questions such as: "What are some of the things that are not working in the way the team functions?" "How would you describe the leadership style of your team leader?" and "What one suggestion would you give your team leader to increase his effectiveness in this position?" The answers the team provided may not have been pleasant for Scott to hear, but they did cause him to stop and think.

It is important for every team, at the beginning of

an alignment, to go through the data-review session described in detail in Chapter 4. This phase of the alignment process becomes even more useful when the leader's dysfunctional style has metastasized throughout the team. The picture presented to Scott was not pretty, since the team described itself by using words such as fractious, abrasive, frustrated, conflicted, unclear, divergent, adversarial, polarized, unaligned, tense, siloed, uncommunicative, ineffective, unfocused, and dysfunctional. These words—and the specific behaviors cited to bring them to life—cut through whatever internal barriers Scott might have erected. Scott was convinced that the moment of truth had arrived when his team members predicted that "if nothing changes in the next five months, the level of frustration and personal dissatisfaction will rise; people will burn out and leave; internal problems will keep the business from moving forward; the organization will fail to achieve its growth targets; the division will lose the credibility and trust of the parent organization and shareholders; it will implode." Change was imperative.

From Rogue to Role Model

The discussion during the initial alignment session was not entirely negative. Scott's team also offered several simple but powerful suggestions to improve the way in which he interacts with them, both individually and as a group. Triangulation was high on the change agenda. The group demanded that, going forward, triangulation no longer be tolerated—no matter who tried it. Issues were to be surfaced and resolved by the parties directly involved—without enlisting a rescuer. Other suggestions for the team's rejuvenated leader included:

- ❏ Assign clear responsibilities to each individual, with no duplication of roles.
- ❏ No more accusing in absentia, and thumbs down to "hands from the grave."
- ❏ Candor during meetings will be a requirement. (Scott's issues and agenda needed to be stated to the team up front; ditto for those of team members.)

Scott is also working with a personal coach to improve his listening skills and his interpersonal style, two factors that had fueled the team's sense of alienation. Meanwhile, according to Sandra, people have begun providing one another with feedback when they display dysfunctional behavior: "There's now an organizational awareness as well as an individual awareness throughout the division." Dysfunctional leadership is giving way to leadership that is strategically focused and forthright, and the new tone is spiraling downward to replace the old.

Leaders as Role Models

When John Doumani stepped into the president's role at Campbell Soup, Asia/Pacific, he found a siloed organization with little, if any, interfunctional communication and cooperation. The organization was a slow-moving behemoth, where getting things done took an eternity. In an industry that depends on being first to market with new products, Campbell could not afford to lose time.

Doumani had learned conflict-management skills and gone through team alignments in prior positions, so he was a strong believer in the power of well-managed conflict. He also knew that he had to start at the top, with his own senior team. Doumani explains how he got the buy-in of this group and, ultimately, the entire organization:

> When I first starting talking to the leadership team about the kind of culture change that I wanted to create, they looked at me like I was from Mars. There was a high level of skepticism, and so my coming in and talking about it meant very little to these people, and rightly so. I tried to explain that one of the most important guidelines we would have to follow was that if a person had an issue, he or she had the right to be heard: to stand up and voice it without any ramifications. A lot of people in the organization didn't believe that, and so I had to model that. I had to encourage people to get up and disagree with me and congratulate them for it instead of punishing them. It wasn't until I had done this several times that they began to believe me. As a leader, you have to do this time and time again: You have to react in a way that reinforces the right behavior, which, in conflict situations, is being open and candid and unafraid.

Doumani knows that behavior is worth a thousand exhortations. It is not what a leader says, but what he or she does that is decisive. We have often been asked to describe the behaviors that senior executives need to model to be able to lead others on the path to effective conflict resolution. Here is a quick list of "Do's" for role-model conflict managers:

DO . . .

1. *Be candid.* When issues surface, put them on the table for discussion.
2. *Be receptive.* Discuss all competing points of view. Let everyone on your team know that it is not only safe to disagree but also expected.
3. *Depersonalize.* Look at each issue that surfaces as a business case, rather than as a personal indictment. (And do let reason triumph over ego.)
4. *Be clear about the decision-making rules of the game.* Will the issue under discussion be decided unilaterally, consultatively, or by consensus?
5. *Outlaw triangulation.* Period!
6. *Learn to listen.* And remember, a key skill here is decoding and feeding back the messages that you think you are hearing. So is "boomerang" questioning, where the leader turns other people's assertions into questions and tosses them back for further elaboration.
7. *Return the monkey to its rightful owner.* Hold executives accountable and ask them to develop solutions. And accept responsibility for the monkeys that are yours.
8. *Recognize and reward successful conflict management when you see it.*

Changing the Leader's Style

An earlier chapter discussed the continuum along which behavior ranges: from nonassertive to assertive to aggressive. When the behavior of the most senior executive falls into one of the two extremes on the continuum, there is certain to be fallout.

Consider the CEO of a $10 billion financial services organization, a nonassertive type who had come up through the ranks and wanted to be one of the group. When an issue surfaced between two executives on his team, he tried to resolve it "through the back door" by meeting separately with each combatant, rather than allowing the issue to run its course to closure. His involvement ensured short-term domestic tranquility, but it also guaranteed that all of the team's problems would linger behind the scenes. Triangulation was inevitable and, not surprisingly, those problems grew to epic proportions. Before long, the CEO had a mess on his hands.

The nice-guy model of leadership simply does not work. Neither does the aggressive approach. The tough-guy leader typically carries baggage that is unsuited for building a high-performance management team, such as being controlling, unreceptive to feedback, and intimidating. In situations like these, top teams often remain stuck in stage one of the team-development wheel, where the members are afraid to confront issues or individuals. Or they may make it to stage two, where members tend to personalize issues, point fingers, and feel attacked. In this case, either bombs go bursting in air, and there is overt conflict as members model the leader's behavior, or all the intrigue of triangulation sets in as they attempt to win the leader's favor.

Julia Nenke, former human resources director for Foxtel, has had firsthand experience with the second type of leader. One general manager with whom she worked in the past epitomized the aggressive leader. Not only was he inclined to "going postal" when things did not go his way, but his reactions were completely unpredictable. If he did not care about an issue—and his team never knew when this was the case—he let people make decisions completely on their own. But if the issue was one of his hot buttons, he brooked no interference: He and he alone made the decision. The problem was that no one ever knew which issues were the hot buttons. Because they never knew how he would react to their suggestions, the members of his team quickly went mute. They became the stage-one team *par excellence.*

How do you, as a leader, know when your behavior is too far to the left or right of the continuum? Most nonassertive leaders realize their need to dial up their behavior, but aggressive leaders are often unaware of how they come across to other people. Roy Anise, senior vice president of planning and information at Phillip Morris, U.S.A., realized that he tended to be very directive with employees and had trouble connecting with them, but when he and his team went through an alignment session, he was surprised to learn that his employees judged him to be far more aggressive than he believed he was. He now understands that his ability to communicate needed honing and that he was overly preoccupied with business results. Anise received similar feedback from his boss, which spurred him to seek coaching.

During his first session with the coach, Anise explained that, as a leader, he was unsure of how his team was progressing and where he needed to take it next. Anise's statement prompted the coach to comment, "Now I know why you are so intimidating." "What are you talking about? I haven't said anything to you," countered Anise. "That's exactly the point," replied the coach. "You keep your cards so close to the chest, so covered up, that I have no idea what you're thinking and what's going on with you. I can see why people who work for you would feel the same sense of not knowing what's going on with you. I can see why they're intimidated."

Anise bristled at the exchange. But a day later, he contacted the coach to thank him for his insight. The coach, of course, had simply been mirroring his pupil's behavior, which had caused Anise to see the light. As Anise said about his coach, "He exposed me and initially I didn't like it, but I needed to hear it."

Once Anise had seen himself as others saw him, he could begin making changes. In one of the exercises his coach used, Anise was asked to imagine various situations that he might find himself in, and where conflict might arise: with direct reports, peers, or superiors. Then, they discussed the impact Anise's current style would have in each situation and how he could bring about a more desirable outcome by consciously becoming less aggressive and more assertive. This scrimmage in consequence thinking was a way of preparing Anise for future encounters with his top team.

Making Change Stick

An earlier chapter introduced Susan Fullman, corporate vice president and director of customer solutions and support for Motorola. Fullman worked hard to tone down her image as a superefficient, no-nonsense manager who had little time for the niceties. Her efforts to solicit other people's opinions, truly listen to them, and engage in a dialogue rather than a monologue changed the tenor of the workplace considerably. As she puts it, "Very little changed, except me, but things are entirely different as a result."

In many ways, changing one's personal style goes against nature—or at least nurture. We have been communicating since we uttered our first cry—and our style has been reinforced, or we would have abandoned it long ago. Personal style does not change overnight or permanently: We are bound to backslide now and then, and it helps to have a plan in place to deal with those moments of regression.

Feedback is one of the best methods of correction. But for many leaders, asking for—and accepting—honest feedback is alien and uncomfortable. After all, it is always easier to dish it out than to receive it. But for those leaders who have made the commitment to change, the payback is substantial. Roy Anise comments:

> During the team alignment, we talked about my aggressive style, and I asked the group to keep me honest: to give me candid feedback if I revert to my old, aggressive style. And they do. They don't allow me to monopolize our meetings or force my opinions on them. When they see my aggressive tendencies returning, they challenge me. As a result, there's been a tremendous increase in openness, enthusiasm, and accountability—not only on the top team but throughout the company. We conduct internal surveys every year, and we've been able to chart the improvement in everything from employee morale to internal customer service.

Before Julia Nenke joined Foxtel, she was vice president of organizational development at Australian food manufacturer Goodman Fielder, where she reported to John Doumani. Nenke was impressed that Doumani genuinely sought and accepted feedback on his own performance. "To do that on an authentic level," she says, "when you are, in fact, at the top of the food chain, provides a terrific model for others to follow."

Leaders must also remain vigilant, on their own account, if they want to avoid backsliding into an ineffective style. One vice president recalls a conversation she had with her coach, in which she revealed that, after returning from an extended vacation, she was having trouble executing the new behaviors she had been learning to internalize before she went away. The coach responded, "You need to think about these behaviors as though they were a blouse that you put on every morning. They need to become part of your daily routine, something that you don't think about at all, that is completely intuitive." The image of waking up in the morning and slipping on these new behaviors stuck in the mind of the vice president, and she conjures it up at the beginning of each day. It helps, she says, "because I am trying to teach an old dog new tricks, and it's very easy for old dogs to return to their old tricks."

The New Leadership Imperative: Letting Go

Senior managers are paid, first and foremost, to get results by working through others. But often they are dragged into the operational fray by employees who are reluctant to assume decision-making responsibility. Although playing Solomon might be an ego trip, it opens up the floodgates. As more managers realize that they can pass the buck back up to the top, a culture of dependency and nonaccountability takes hold. Small wonder that little time is left for strategic thinking.

Effective leaders refuse to be drawn into the dependency trap. When Linda Woltz became president of Sara Lee Underwear, she moved to shift the culture from one that viewed the leader as the ultimate handler of disputes to one in which senior executives and those below them took on that responsibility. When a dispute is brought before her, she asks, "Who are the players who need to be brought together to resolve this issue?" She provides whatever support may be needed to get them together, leaves them alone, and expects them to inform her only of the results.

Another quality that Julia Nenke continues to admire in her

old boss, John Doumani, is his ability to distinguish between those issues in which he needs to become involved and those that should be left to others to resolve. She explains:

> His reaction differs from the normal reaction of most leaders who, when an issue is presented to them, immediately assume that they should take a role and have an opinion, no matter what the issue. John has the maturity and technique to stand back, even if he has a point of view or a preference for the way it should be played out. He really believes that it is more important to instill accountability in the members of his team than for him to be heard. Because he refuses to offer a solution, his team is forced to jump in and resolve issues by themselves.

Nenke herself devoted time to working with her team at Foxtel to identify, prioritize, and assign responsibility for issues. Putting each issue into the "right box," as she calls it, enabled Nenke to quickly determine which were strategic in nature—"the big things" that required her involvement—and which could be handled at a lower level.

One Style Does Not Fit All

Accountability for resolving an issue between top executives lies, in the first instance, with them. But astute leaders have a laserlike ability to focus on the capabilities of their top team. Realizing that not every team member is at the same stage on the team-development wheel, they choose to be more—or less—directive, as needed.

In working with the members of their team, leaders can adopt one of four general styles:[4]

1. They can be *directive* and tell employees the what, where, when, and how of an issue.
2. They can *coach*, deemphasizing the "how" in favor of the "why."
3. They can choose to be *collaborative,* and treat their senior team members as partners.
4. They can choose to *delegate,* allowing team members to run with the ball.

Each style has its advantages, and each is appropriate in a different situation. Lew Frankfort, CEO and chairman of Coach, Inc., explains how and when he varies his style:

> I try to be on the alert for ways to maximize my effectiveness with each person I work with, based on the situation at hand. My style with each of my teams varies based on the situation and my relationship with my people. In some cases I feel very comfortable saying, "I'm telling you to do this." I often choose this style when we need to move rapidly, and I am very clear about what needs to be accomplished, while the other people who are involved don't have the broader view. At other times, I decide to hang back, maybe to participate, but to let others take the lead. For instance, if a person is really expert in his or her field, I don't need to do much more than provide an understanding of goals and some oversight. I also consider coaching, or mentoring, to be one of my most important

roles. I coach in many ways: by modeling behavior; by consistently using rigor and logic to make decisions; by setting realistic, firm expectations; and by providing critical feedback—both constructive criticism when a person is underperforming and appreciation when they have been successful.

Let's examine in greater detail when and why a leader would opt for each style.

Directing

Directing has a long pedigree. In the old, vertical organization, orders came down from higher up and were expected to be carried out with few questions. In today's horizontal organization, leaders of high-performance teams at every level are somewhat akin to the prime minister of England vis-à-vis the cabinet: They remain *primus inter pares*—first among equals. The ability to influence—to persuade others to change their points of view and behaviors so that they are aligned with yours—has become a critical skill. Today's leaders must command respect without commanding. Given this new paradigm and the complexity of the modern enterprise, effective leaders are gravitating increasingly toward assuming the roles of coach and delegator.

There are, however, times when a leader must be directive. For example, the CEO is ultimately the one who is responsible for the strategic well-being of the organization. If there is a directional dispute within the top-management team, he or she is obliged to listen to all sides. But when action is needed, the CEO must make the tough choice rather than allow strategic disagreement to go unresolved.

Even at an operational level, leaders at times must be directive. For example, when a new vice president of marketing comes into the company from an entirely different industry, he or she may lack the technical knowledge necessary to make decisions related to the company's product lines. Or, when a person has moved from one function to another, the leader might need to step in and shore up shallow knowledge or lack of experience.

Sometimes it is obvious from the questions the person asks that additional direction is required before the task can be carried out or the decision made. In other cases, the leader may need to test the person's capabilities with questions such as:

❐ What experience have you had working with _____?

❐ When you had a project similar to _____, what were the first steps you took to get it rolling? How would you begin to get this project going?

❐ When you put together task forces in the past, how did you decide who should be on the team? Who would you want on the team for this project?

❐ When you were looking for information on _____, where did you look for it? Where would you look for information on this project?

❐ In the past, when conflict came up on your team, how did you deal with it? How will you deal with it if it comes up during this project?

The responses to these and other capability-testing questions tell the leader a great deal about the employee's ability to work independently and about the degree of direction that will be needed.

Coaching

Even in situations where employees possess the ability and willingness to step up to increased responsibility, leaders must proceed cautiously. Before leaders can legitimately hold people accountable for solving problems, making decisions, and managing conflict, they must ratchet up the level of competency. By coaching employees through tough issues, leaders help them to develop the skills they will need to operate effectively on their own.

One of the most effective coaching techniques is the use of so-called boomerang questions. After the person answers one question, the leader turns that statement into another question, and the answer to that question into another question, and so on. The objective is to encourage the person to look beneath the surface of the issue, to explore every avenue, before arriving at a decision.

A highly skilled manager at Motorola U.S. used boomerang questions to help one of his team members resolve an issue with a colleague in Europe. The U.S. manager and his team were in charge of developing a worldwide plan for introducing a new product. But the data that the team required from the European manager had not been received, in spite of numerous requests. The American was completely frustrated when he began complaining to his superior. The conversation went something like this:

LEADER: "What do you see as the next steps?"

TEAM MEMBER: "I can just move ahead on my own."

LEADER: "Could you elaborate on that? When you say you'll move ahead on your own, what exactly do you mean?"

TEAM MEMBER: "We'll write up the plan and start executing without him."

LEADER: "What are the pros and cons of doing that?

TEAM MEMBER: "I'll get it done, but I'll alienate the folks in Europe."

LEADER: "Do you have any other options?"

TEAM MEMBER: "I can tell the rest of the European team that we can't wait any longer. We've got to move ahead, so let's discuss it in a conference call."

LEADER: "What are the pros and cons of this option?"

TEAM MEMBER: "It will get them on board, but it will slow us down, and it may not resolve the issue."

LEADER: "Do you have any other options?"

TEAM MEMBER: "Yes, we can engage in a 'conflict conversation' (part of Motorola's conflict-resolution protocols). I'd say we need to escalate this to the team."

As it turned out, the issue between the two managers was brought to the attention of the team. It was discussed at the next team meeting and resolved speedily.

One key to effective coaching is to refuse to be drawn into the content trap. Once a leader becomes entangled in the details of an issue, it becomes difficult to resist the temptation to start giving advice and offering solutions, which completely defeats the purpose of coaching. Here, there is an obvious parallel with the old saying, "Give a man a fish and you feed him for a day; teach him how to fish and you feed him for a lifetime." Give an employee a solution and you enable that person to resolve a specific issue, but teach an employee how to arrive at solutions and you enable that person to resolve future issues.

Leaders who are committed to passing on analytical-thinking skills do not focus on content questions such as "What will happen if you have to go into overtime to meet the deadline?" or "How long will it take ship the new packages to Europe?"

keeping me from making this change?" and "Why?" Self-examination may be sufficient for breaking through the barrier; if not, personal coaching may be necessary.

Giving Feedback: Ground Rules for Leaders

Effective feedback is key to effective conflict management. This book has discussed the importance of surveying team members before an alignment session and then feeding the results back to them. This practice holds up the mirror of objectivity. Feedback is also a critical part of self-assessment exercises: Asking individuals to characterize themselves in terms of their communication style—nonassertive, assertive, or aggressive—then asking their teammates to give them feedback is a reality check. When teaching active listening skills, we stress the importance of decoding and feeding back messages to the listener to ensure that both parties agree on the factual and emotional issues that need to be addressed.

Feedback, according to Michael Carey, corporate vice president of human resources at Johnson & Johnson, is akin to "shining a hot, white light" on an organization's interpersonal dynamics. It surfaces issues, opens up opportunities for discussion and improvement, and, when delivered constructively, is one of the best deterrents to dysfunctional conflict.

How, When, Where, and to What Degree?

These are straightforward questions, but they are often overlooked. Ask them, and the answers you get will help you to choose the right time and venue for feedback sessions and to develop the right script. Remember Scott from the case study, whose behavior upset and offended the members of his team? One of the major issues they had with him was his tendency to berate them publicly, without giving them the opportunity to refute the charges leveled against them. During the alignment, the subteam that he had directed to formulate strategy, then second-guessed, were vocal about how belittled and embarrassed they had felt by Scott's surprise feedback in front of the management committee.

Attending behaviors are the things a listener does to convey the following message to a speaker: "I really want to hear what you have to say, and I'll be 'all ears' when we sit down for a discussion." One attending behavior that is critical to active listening is paying attention to time and place, and it is equally important when giving feedback. While there are instances where on-the-spot, public feedback is necessary, in most cases, dedicated time and privacy are more appropriate. Most leaders hold tightly to this rule when conducting scheduled performance reviews, but often forget it when giving informal, unscheduled feedback.

One effective leader always begins unscheduled feedback sessions by asking, "Is this a good time for me to give you some feedback?" Asking the question eliminates possible distractions and keeps his direct reports from feeling as though they are being taken by surprise. If the answer he receives is no, he ensures that a more appropriate time is scheduled for the feedback session.

Human resources literature is full of advice about giving feedback, so it is not necessary to dwell here on such issues as ensuring that you give both positive and negative feedback, how to order and balance the two, and the need to provide rewards and recognition. But one area tends to be overlooked: Every feedback session should be a two-way street.

Too often, leaders focus solely on giving feedback and neglect to engage in discussion with the person who is being evaluated. One way to do this is to provide equal time for a response. "What's *your* perception?" "Do you have any feedback for *me* about how *I've* handled this issue?" These questions can open the door to a very meaningful conversation.

One chief information officer (CIO) delivered a message to her information services director that she had received only one progress report in the first month of their organization's ERP (enterprise resource planning) system installation. She did not believe that she was being kept informed. "What's your take on the situation?" the CIO asked engagingly. The IS director pointed out that the two of them had never agreed on a reporting schedule, and he had thought that a monthly update would be sufficient. Opening the dialogue during the feedback session allowed the two to resolve the issue, which was to contract for the leader to receive biweekly reports from then on. The feedback session was concluded with no hard feelings and with an effective business solution in place.

When soliciting a response after delivering feedback, effective leaders employ the active listening skills discussed in Chapter 5, especially those that relate to decoding the emotional message behind the response. For example, suppose one of your employees continually shows up late for meetings. You arrange a meeting to discuss her tardiness. She explains that she is always swamped and cannot break away in time. Do not let the conversation stop there. It may be that she is engaging in passive-aggressive behavior as a substitute for addressing a deeper issue. To get to the root cause, use probing techniques such as "say more" responses ("Tell me more about the distribution of work in your department"), paraphrasing ("You seem to be saying that you have too much work to handle"), and decoding and feeding back ("You seem angry about the amount of work that's been assigned to you").

Feedback: A Front-Line Perspective

Paul Michaels has thought long and hard about the art and discipline of feedback. It is a mechanism he uses to motivate and lead others as well as to foster group cohesiveness, mutual respect, and support. Although he believes that there is no silver bullet for how leaders should provide and receive feedback, his insights, drawn from years of experience, are sharp and worth considering. We sought his expertise for answering the following questions:

QUESTION: "Is feedback an art, a science, or a discipline?"

MICHAELS: "Unlike a lot of managers, I don't think giving feedback is 'a delicate art.' In fact, I think it's a lot like digging trenches: You've got to put lots of muscle into it, day after day."

QUESTION: "How often should a leader provide feedback?"

MICHAELS: "I believe the best leaders don't give people feedback once a quarter or even once a month. Sure, formal evaluation and performance discussions should be conducted several times a year. However, I give my team members feedback and informal coaching every day. When you don't have time to give feedback, you're really saying you don't have time to lead."

QUESTION: "Is there a distinction between giving feedback to high performers and to underachievers?"

MICHAELS: "Interestingly, my direct reports not only don't dread feedback, they actually solicit it. I've found that it's usually the highest-performing employees who are most apt to seek feedback. They are looking to improve. But the people who are insecure avoid feedback. They pretend that they know everything already and don't need anyone else's opinion. With these people, you have to get across the message that not knowing everything and asking others for feedback is perfectly natural and acceptable."

QUESTION: "What's your best advice to leaders about how to give feedback?"

MICHAELS: "People rarely come into management possessing all the knowledge, skills, and abilities necessary to advance. They must develop, and it's a leader's responsibility to develop the next generation of leaders. Feedback has to be timely and very specific. If somebody does something that is not in line with their potential, you don't wait a month or three months or until their annual review to tell them about it. You pull them into a room right away and say, 'Look, when you did this, when you acted this way, I didn't like it, and this is why.'"

QUESTION: "Anything else?"

MICHAELS: "I like to deliver feedback with clarity, candor, and insight—and a little bit of humor helps. Basically, you reiterate your expectations, and just as you share coaching on how to improve, you also tell your people how proud you are when they exceed expectations. Communicate what the consequences will be if the unacceptable behavior continues. The more direct you are, the better. I'm not talking about threatening or passing judgment on the person's character. But view the situation as a business issue that needs to be resolved: 'Here's what has to change; here's what will happen if it doesn't; here's when we'll meet again to review your progress.' The goal is to have people work more effectively, develop new skills, and grow professionally."

QUESTION: "But being direct can be threatening, can't it?"

MICHAELS: "We tend to go lightly when providing feedback because we are afraid of hurting people's feelings.
But, in my experience, people aren't as thin-skinned as
we think. In fact, some of them are so thick-skinned
that you have to make your point over and over. Then
you have to ask them to repeat it back to you several
times to make sure they've gotten it. We've probably all
worked for someone who was direct, as well as for
someone who avoided 'tough' conversations. People
usually prefer to know where they stand and trust a
leader who is willing to give them the unvarnished
truth. You lose credibility if you are not willing to address a performance issue as well as recognize the wins."

QUESTION: "And the payoff?"

MICHAELS: "It's very hard to give people honest feedback,
but it's so worth it. There is nothing more exciting or
more fun than to watch somebody to whom you've
given tough feedback really respond, address the issue,
and show improvement. There's nothing more hearten-
ing, exciting, and rewarding for both of you!"

The Leader as "Dealer"

Effective leaders know when to hold them and when to fold
them. Take John Doumani. He is a tenacious leader who would
move mountains to retain an executive whom he feels has high
potential. He has personally coached many executives whose
conflict-resolution skills were iffy, at best, and transformed
them into effective team players. Recently, the aggressive style
of one young manager—who in another organization might
have been rewarded for his seemingly strong and decisive

ways—was troubling to Doumani. Concerned that this young man's arrogance was alienating other people and would lead to bigger problems, Doumani told the rest of the team that they owed it to the executive and the organization to give him honest feedback about his style and provide him with the skills to change.

The senior team, his divisional head, and his functional head did exactly that. The latter took the lead in obtaining individual coaching for the executive who, as a result, has succeeded in turning around his behavior.

But even Doumani is occasionally unsuccessful; he recently described a situation with a different outcome. One of his functional heads was departing after two years with the company. During those two years, the executive had received a good deal of negative feedback. Members of the function had complained to human resources about his failure to deal with poor performers on the team, his refusal to consider changing the inefficient structure of the department, and so on. Other members of the leadership team had problems with lack of strategic thinking vis-à-vis his function and with his personal style.

After the feedback and attempts at coaching brought about no change, Doumani met with the employee one final time before he left to convey a strong message. Here is how Doumani described that meeting:

> My point to him was very clear: "No matter how good a job you are doing technically, if you don't address the issues related to the leadership of your function, I can't have you here." We put together a plan outlining what he wanted to do with the department. I coached him through that, and then I said, "We have to sit down in six months' time and judge the progress you've made on this plan. At that time you will solicit

360-degree feedback on your progress, and we
will factor that into our discussion." I also told
him that my biggest worry was that he didn't
seem to be aware of the extent of the problems:
He always seemed to be wearing rose-colored
glasses. I told him I was going to assign him a
mentor: somebody who would work with him
through the next six months and whom he could
use to get feedback as to how he was doing—
because I was afraid he wouldn't see it himself.

To Doumani's disappointment, neither his coaching nor
the help of the mentor made any difference. Six months later,
nothing had changed, and Doumani made good on his word.
This is a case of a leader having to "fold them."

Honest Leadership

Effective leadership in conflict management requires honesty.
This might sound like motherhood and piety; however, the
news from Enron to Tyco to WorldCom gives us great pause.
Without commitment to total honesty, candor, and openness,
no attempt to manage organizational conflict will succeed. Figure 7-1 lists additional roadblocks that prevent effective conflict
management.

Pat Parenty, senior vice president and general manager of
Redken, U.S.A., sums it up well:

When you make promises, you must deliver on
them or explain why you can't. You can't say to
your team, "I want you guys to be honest with
each other," and then not be honest with them,

Roadblocks to Effective Conflict Management

Many leaders have encountered the following roadblocks during their efforts to improve their organization's or team's conflict-resolution skills. How many are operative in your environment?

The Dependency Story
A surprising number of executives still adhere to the leadership story that "theirs is not to reason why; it's up to the leader to do or die." Such leaders must redefine their role and change the going-in story that they and they alone have the power and accountability to resolve issues.

Managing by Tantrum
Public displays of rage prompt people to go underground. People look at targets of such rage and project, "This could be happening to me." Any hope the leader ever had of getting honest opinions and feedback from them is effectively killed.

One Style Fits All
It is easy for a leader to manage by whatever leadership style he or she feels is most comfortable. But effective leaders match their style—directing, coaching, collaborating, or delegating—to the learning curve of their employees.

One-Dimensional Leadership
No one would argue with a focus on business results. But raising the question, "How well are we doing?" should not stop with the financials. It should also encompass accountabilities and alignment. Do senior executives see themselves accountable for the whole "game," rather than only for their function? Is the organization aligned level to level, cross-functionally, and interfunctionally? Dysfunctional conflict tends to erupt where there is a lack of alignment.

Figure 7-1. Roadblocks to effective conflict management.

not put the issues on the table, whether they're
good, bad, or indifferent. You also have to share
with the team members all the facts they will
need in order to make the right decision. If there
are sacred cows or taboo areas and you don't tell
them, they may make a decision that will get you
all in trouble. You must trust them with confidential information; if you can't do that, you
have no business asking them to take responsibility. You must give honest feedback, no matter
how painful it may be. And, most of all, when
you tell your team that you want them to be totally honest with you, you must mean it.

Litmus Test for Leaders

Are there any tools leaders can use to test their personal profi-
ciency at managing top-team conflict? Over the years, we have
put together a set of questions designed to help leaders assess
how well their actions support the evolution of a high-performance team and minimize conflict. Ask yourself:

Have I, as a leader, ensured that . . .

- ❒ The missions and goals of the team are clear to all members?
- ❒ The team has the correct players—those who are both
  technically and functionally competent and possess the
  ability and willingness to do their job?
- ❒ Roles and points of intersection/turf are clear to all
  members of the team?
- ❒ Team members are committed to a winning team instead
  of to their own parochial/functional self-interest?

❐ The decision-making/leadership approach that the team employs is understood and accepted by all team members?

❐ Every team member feels a sense of ownership/accountability for the business results that the team creates?

❐ All team members are comfortable dealing with conflict in the team?

❐ The team is willing to periodically self-assess its progress as a group, focusing on how well they handle conflict situations?

❐ Constructive feedback to team members is always provided at an appropriate time and place and in an appropriate manner?

❐ Two-way feedback is promoted—and listened to?

❐ Good conflict-management behavior and skills—openness, candor, depersonalization, active listening, and situational leadership styles—are part of my leadership repertoire.

End Note

Sometimes the team must take charge. This chapter has focused on the pivotal role of leaders in managing conflict. This emphasis is justified, because the leader is—or should be—at the forefront of organizational change.

But be clear about this point: Teams, especially senior-management teams, cannot abdicate responsibility for change. Leaders need prodding, especially when those below are aware of the need for change before it enters the consciousness of the CEO, divisional president, department head, or plant manager.

The anonymous teams we've talked about—such as "Art's

team" and "Scott's team"—were dissatisfied with the status quo but endured their leader's maladaptive behavior for a long time before addressing it. In popular psychological parlance, they can be called enablers or codependents. They certainly were not owners or board members.

It is the responsibility of every team to challenge the leader, especially in the face of unresolved conflict. True, it helps when the leader is a proficient conflict manager. But not all leaders are, and in those cases, it is the team that must take the lead.

Being a member of the team—a follower, in other words—does not mean that you must be passive. Followers can stand up to the leader; they can take positions on issues; they can help clarify agendas; they can assume responsibility for making things happen. To do otherwise might postpone the inevitable clash of the Goliaths, but it also delays, perhaps permanently, the opportunity to turn top-team conflict into high performance.

Notes

1. Michael Kinsman, "Ignoring Conflict Just Doesn't Work," Copley News Service, March 26, 2001.
2. Edward G. Wertheim, "Leadership: An Overview," http://web.cba. neu.edu/~ewertheim/leader/leader.htm.
3. Ibid.
4. Kenneth Blanchard and Paul Hersey have written extensively on the various styles a leader can adopt. For further details, see Blanchard, Kenneth, and Paul Hersey, *Management of Organizational Behavior: Utilizing Human Resources* (Englewood Cliffs, N.J.: Prentice-Hall, 1982), pp. 82–105.

Index

Abbott Laboratories, 59–60
accommodating (conflict mode),
    136, 137
accountability
    assignment of, 111–112
    for business results, 86–88
    e-mail and avoidance of,
      172–173
    strategic conflict in, 37–43
action, commitment to, 56–57
active listening, 139–152
    attending behavior for,
      145–147
    behaviors and techniques for,
      144–151
    behaviors to avoid in, 141–144
    decoding/feeding back feelings
      in, 149–151
    moving to action from,
      151–152
    paraphrasing in, 148–149
    passive listening as, 147–148
    "say more" responses in, 148
active-reading skills, 183–186
affiliative investment, 29
aggressive style, 17, 53, 152, 153,
    208

agreement, assessing degree of,
    133–135
aligning teams (phase 3),
    120–123
alignment, 33–56
    of business relationships/mu-
      tual expectations, 52–56
    and commitment to action,
      56–57
    of goals/business priorities/
      focus, 34–37
    for high-performance teams,
      66–67
    of individual roles/account-
      ability, 37–43
    key areas of, 33
    of protocols/rules of engage-
      ment, 43–52
Amado, Joe, 36–37
    on handling disputes, 41
    on role alignment, 40
    and role/responsibility clarity,
      39–41
Anise, Roy, 36
    on personal style, 211
    style change by, 209–210

About the Author

Howard M. Guttman is the principal of Guttman Development Strategies, Inc., which was founded in 1989 and is located in Ledgewood, New Jersey. GDS, Inc. is a management consulting firm focusing on the areas of executive development, management development, and organization development in the United States and internationally. With a current staff of sixteen consultants, GDS clients represent a wide range of industries and include Colgate-Palmolive, L'Oréal USA, Sara Lee Corporation, Campbell Soup, HBO, *The New York Times,* Johnson & Johnson, Pfizer, and Motorola.

Guttman's corporate experience includes Johnson & Johnson, where he was director of human resources at Personal Products Co. In this capacity, he was responsible for organization development, management development, employee relations, EEO affirmative action, recruiting, and employee services. Previously, he served as national manager of human resources development and general manager of headquarters personnel at Johnson & Johnson.

Before joining Johnson & Johnson, Guttman was senior organizational development consultant for Automatic Data Processing (ADP). At both Johnson & Johnson and ADP, he specialized in internal consulting, focusing on the development of marketing and sales organizations, team development, total employee involvement, diversity/mentoring, organizational structuring, and leadership training.

Guttman has consulted with numerous Fortune 500 corporations, universities, and nonprofit organizations in the United States and internationally. He has spoken at various professional conferences on topics such as "Executive Development," "Consulting at the Board Level," "Accelerating Organization Development," "Strategic Training Initiatives," and "Cross-Functional Team Development."

Additionally, Guttman frequently appears on television and radio and in the print media, including MSNBC, *New Jersey News 12*, Comcast Network's *One on One*, *The Star Ledger*, WMAQ Chicago, *Management Review Magazine*, and *Business News New Jersey*.

Guttman holds a master's degree from Case Western Reserve University's School of Applied Social Sciences. He was previously affiliated with the Graduate School of Management at Rutgers University as a professor of organization behavior and management consulting. Guttman was also an adjunct professor of behavioral consulting at Fairleigh Dickinson University's Graduate School of Psychology.

- clear roles and responsibilities w/ status report -
- Issue management - reports w/ status report -
- Accountability for decision making

- category teams responsible for conflict resolution

Needs -
- Need to address issues clearly -
- communicate so become shared risk

Accountability Exercise? p. 84
commitment decisions to all reported!
- Purdue self - assessment
Power to reference p. 132
Leadership - p. 207